INDOOR PLANTS & FLOWERS
Adult Coloring Book

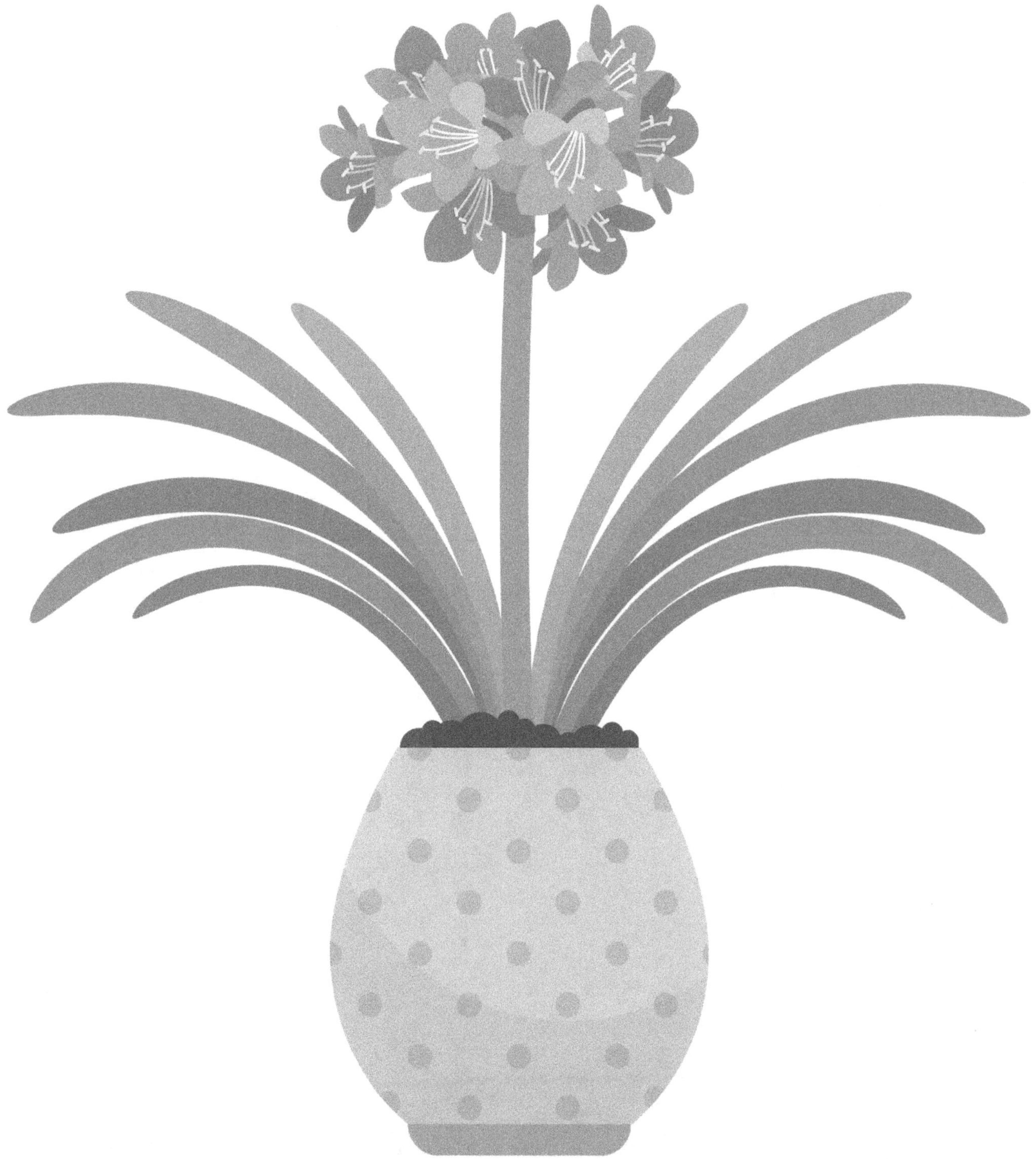

44 Beautiful Designs

Copyright 2020 © Adult Coloring Fun

All rights reserved

No part of this book may be reproduce or used in any form without the written consent of the author and publisher.

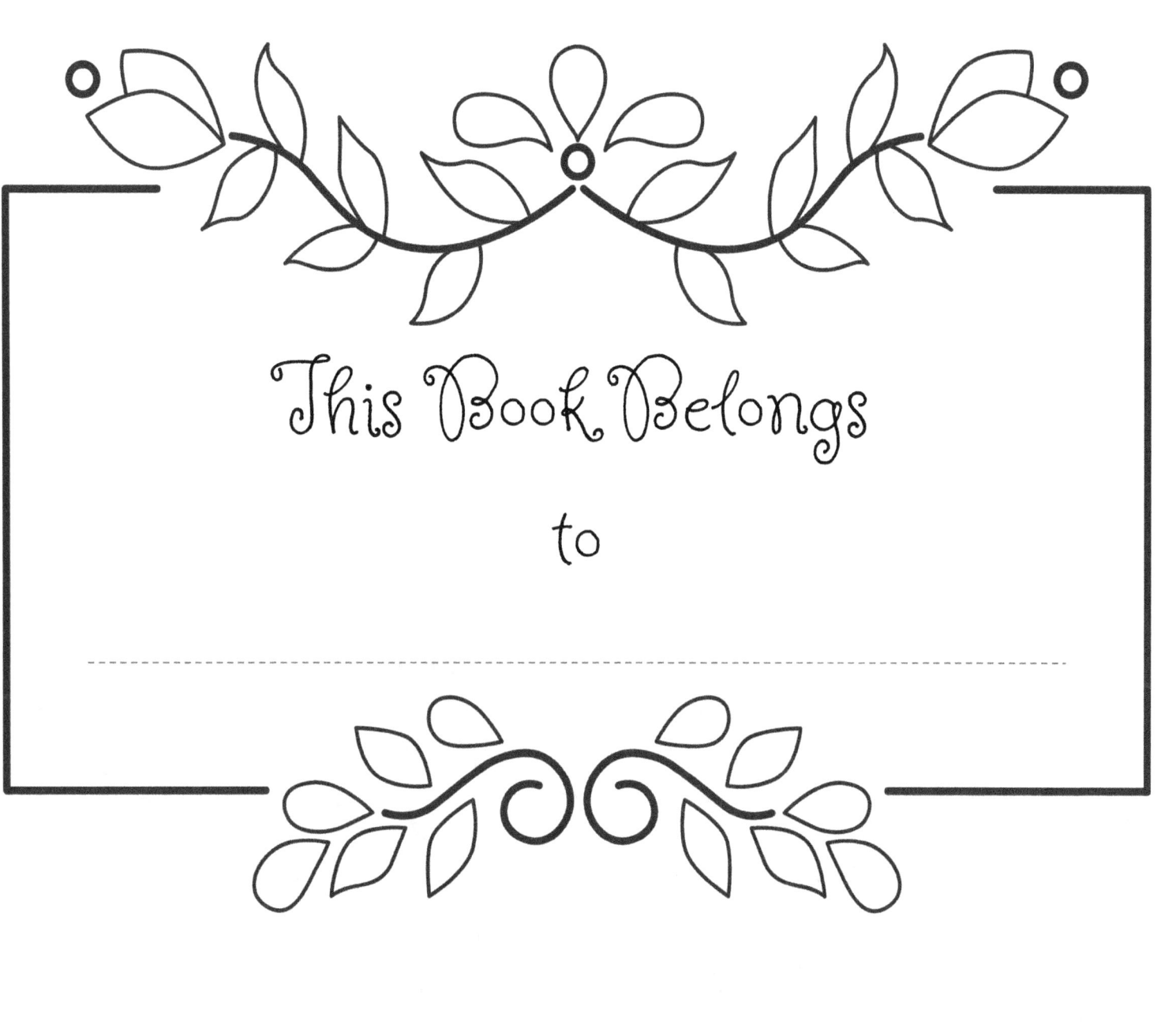

Color Test

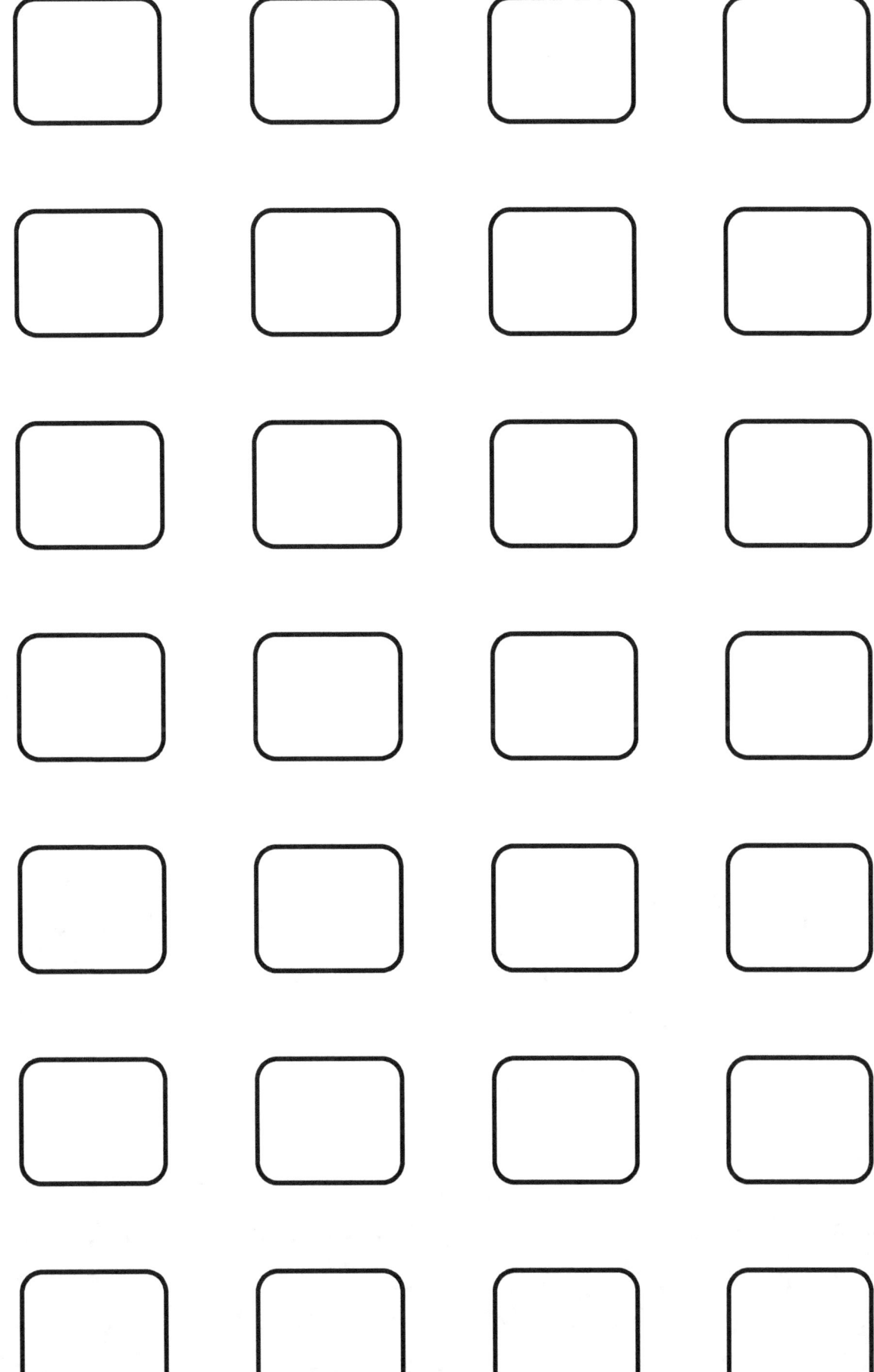

Primrose

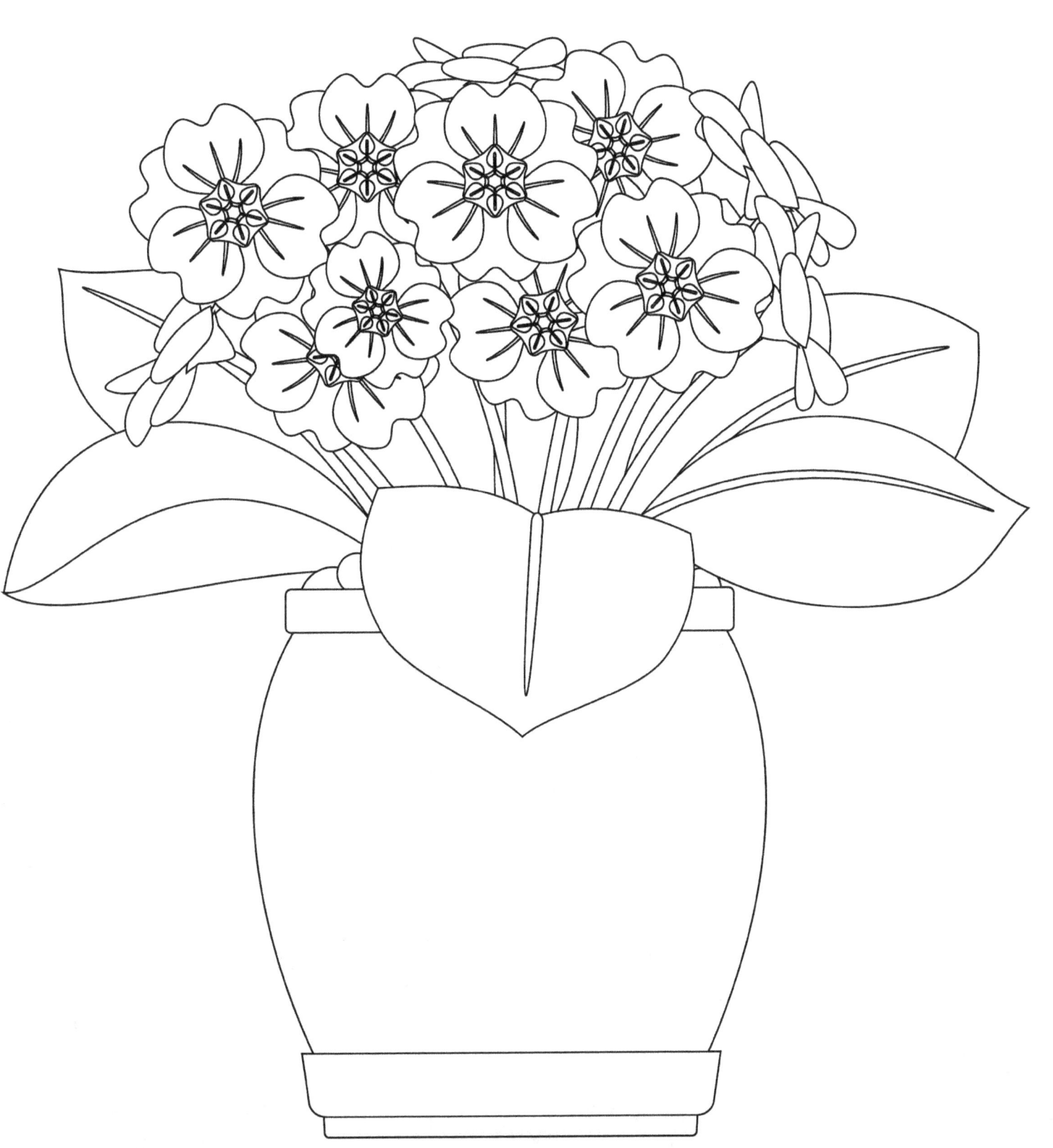

Alocasia

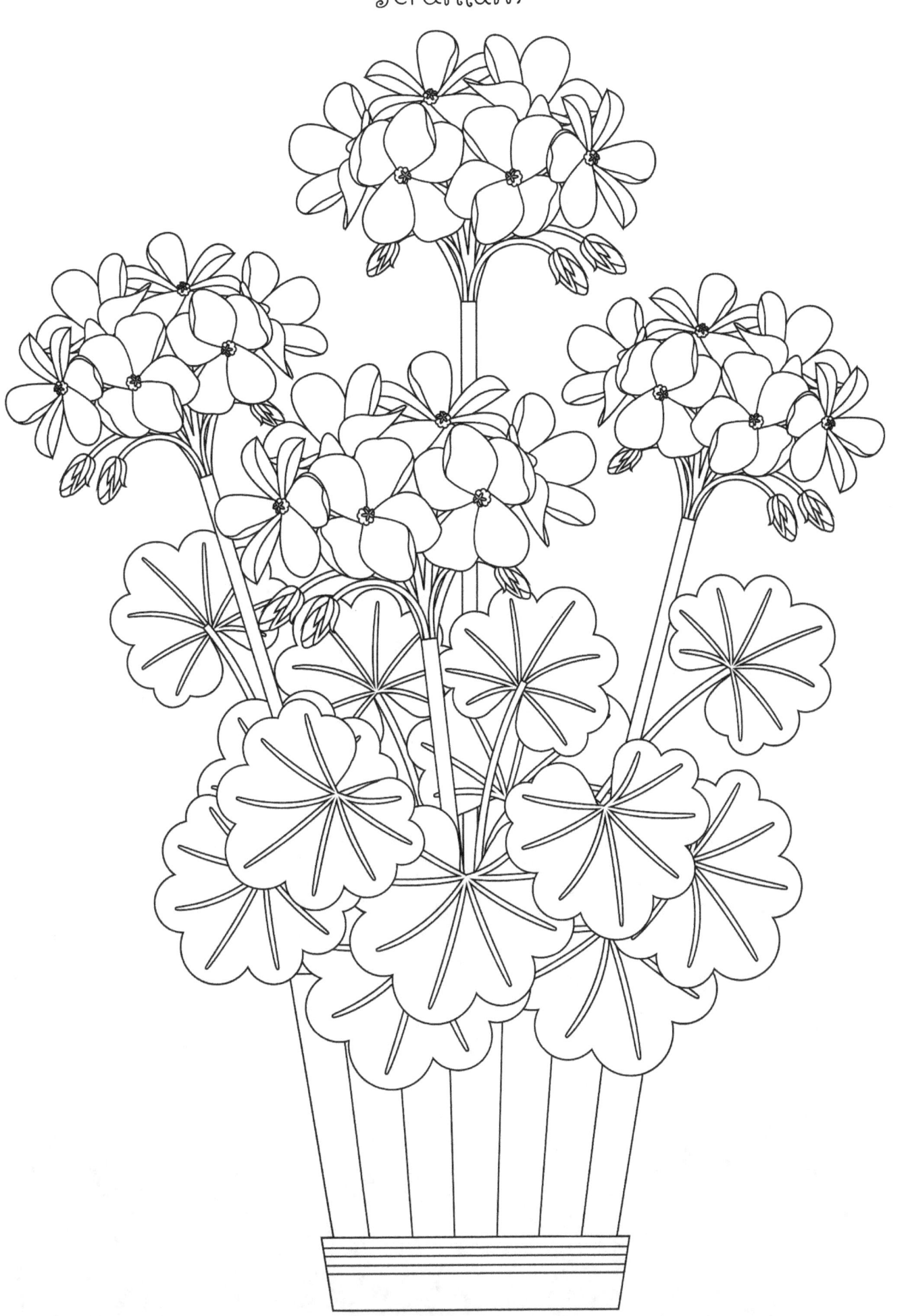

Heart Of Jesus

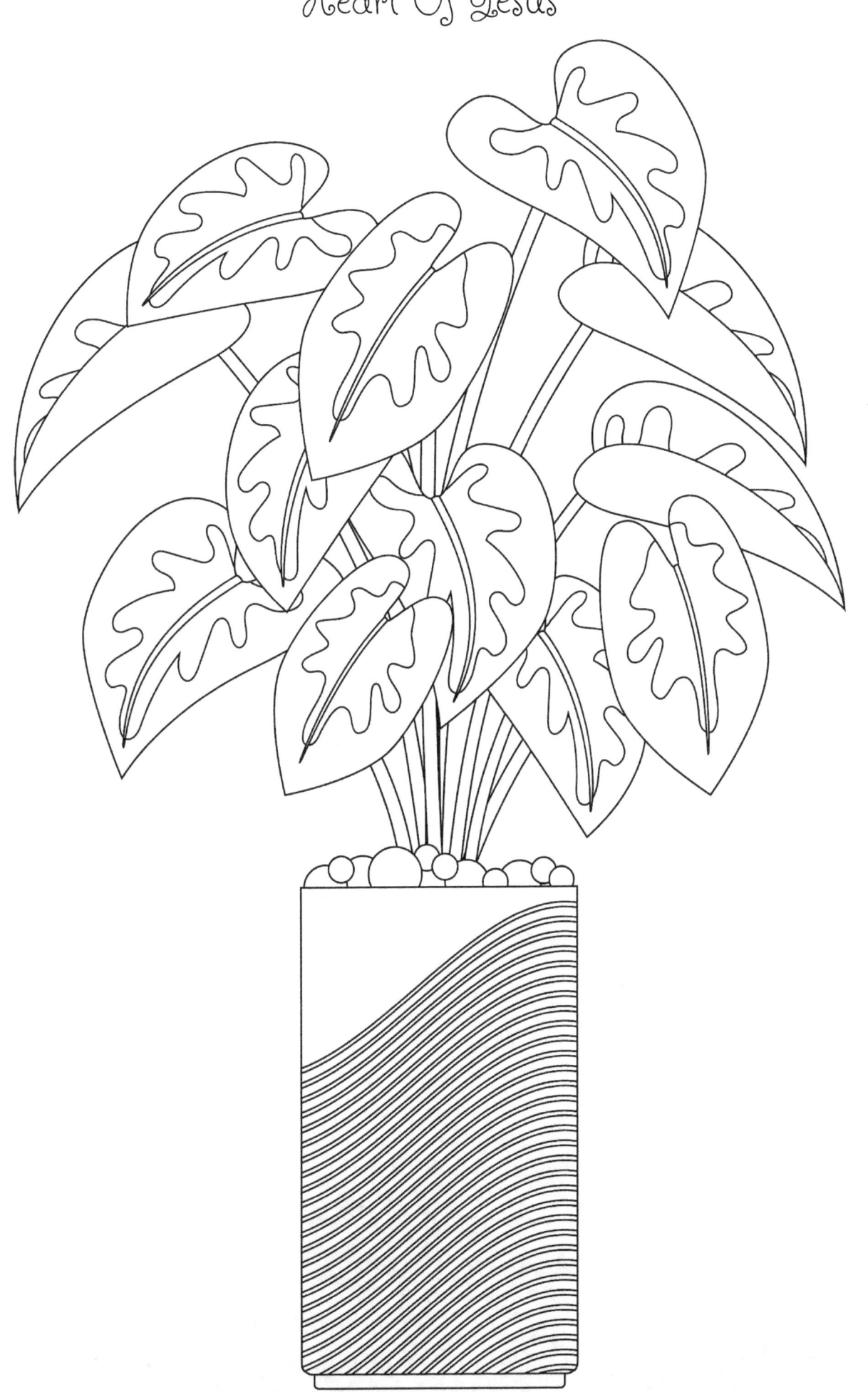

Hydrangea

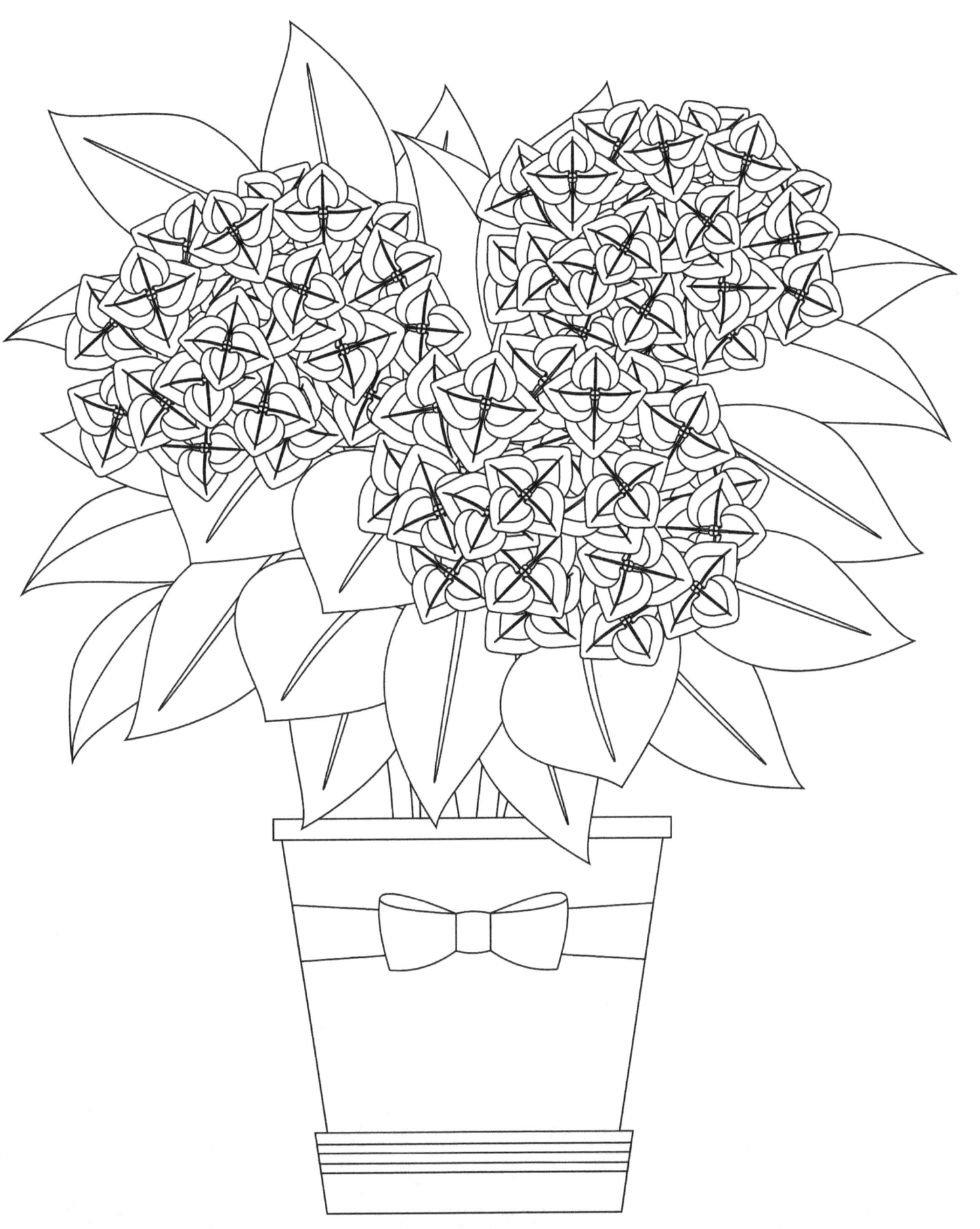

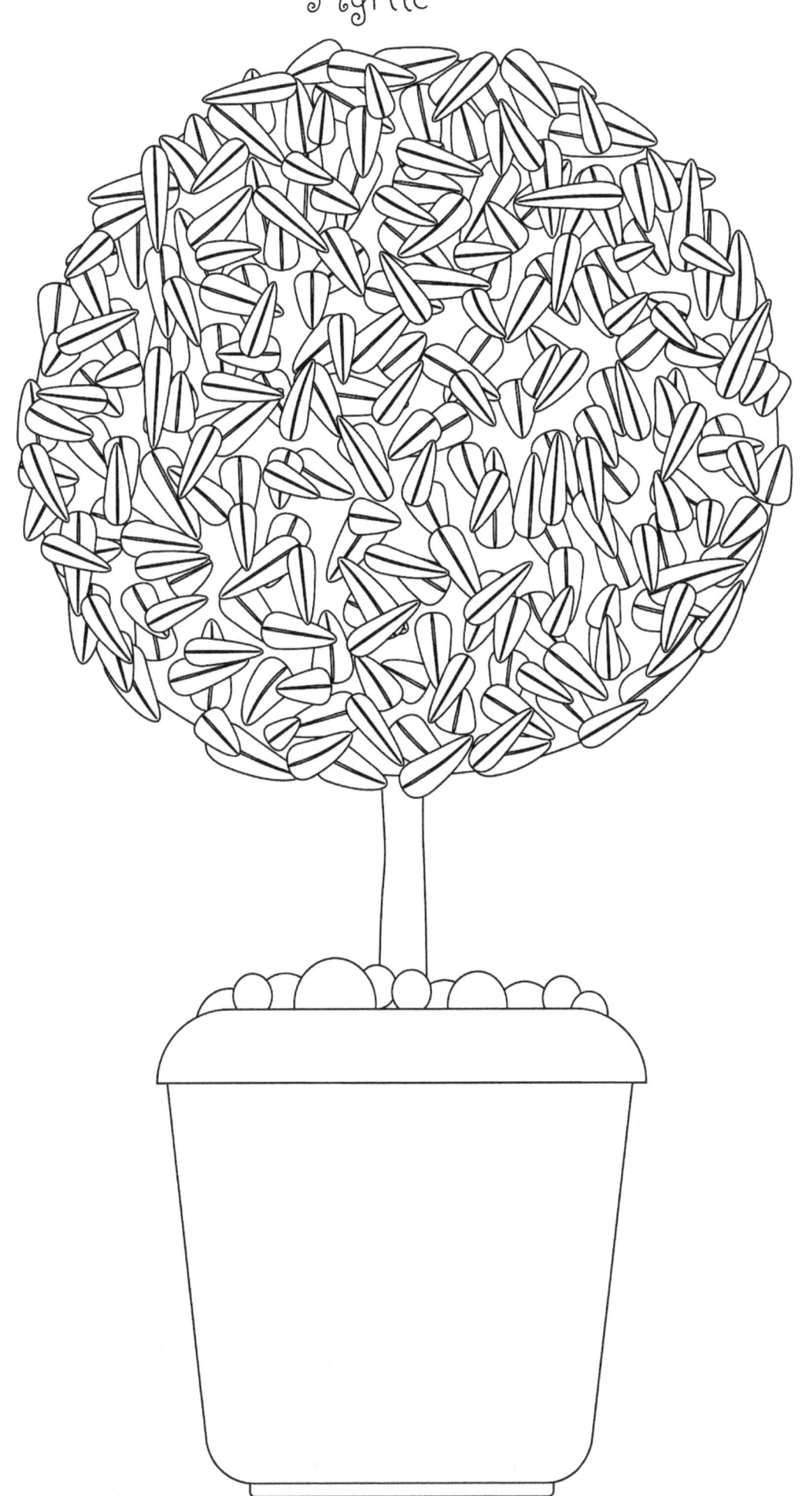

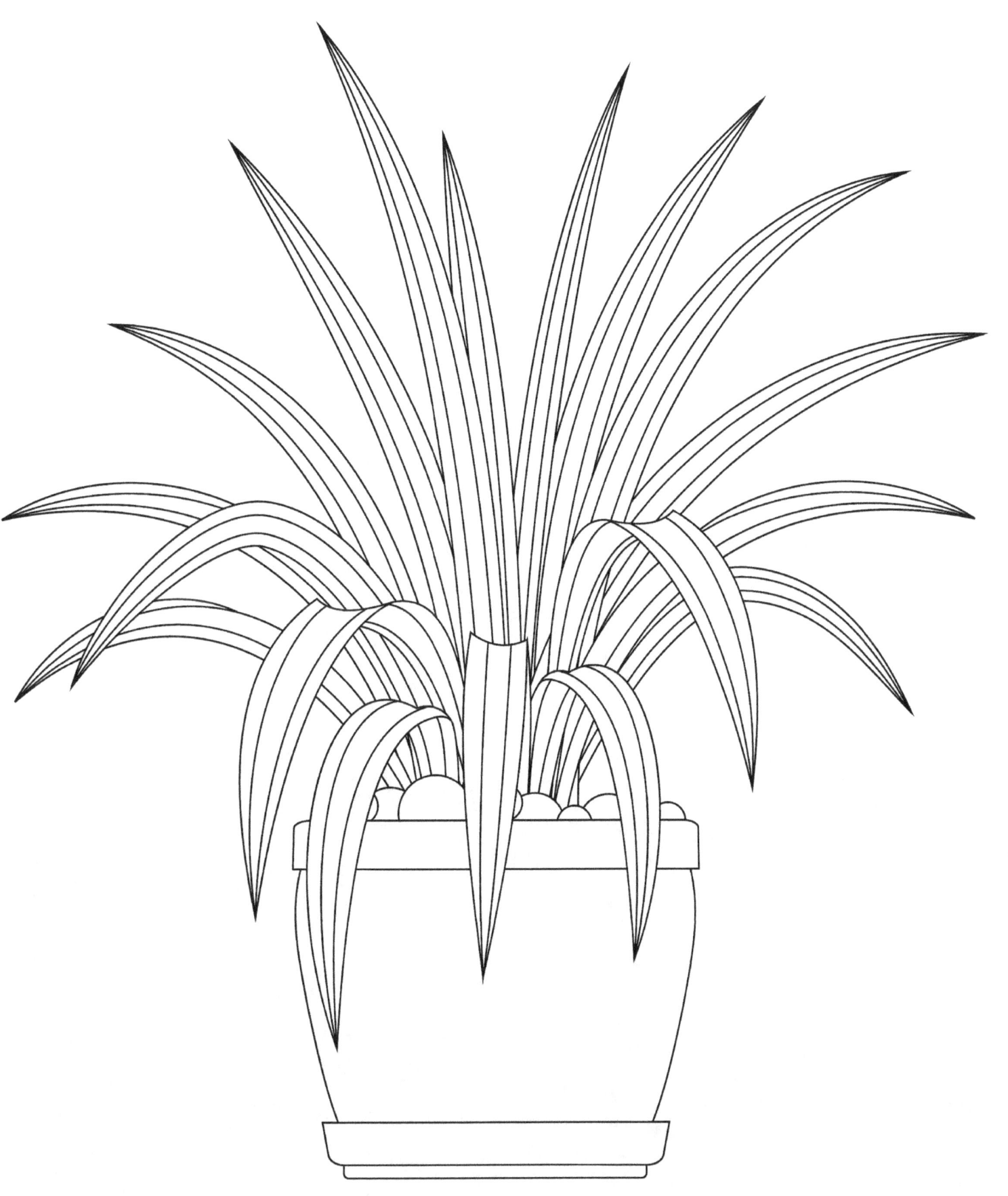

Bush Lily

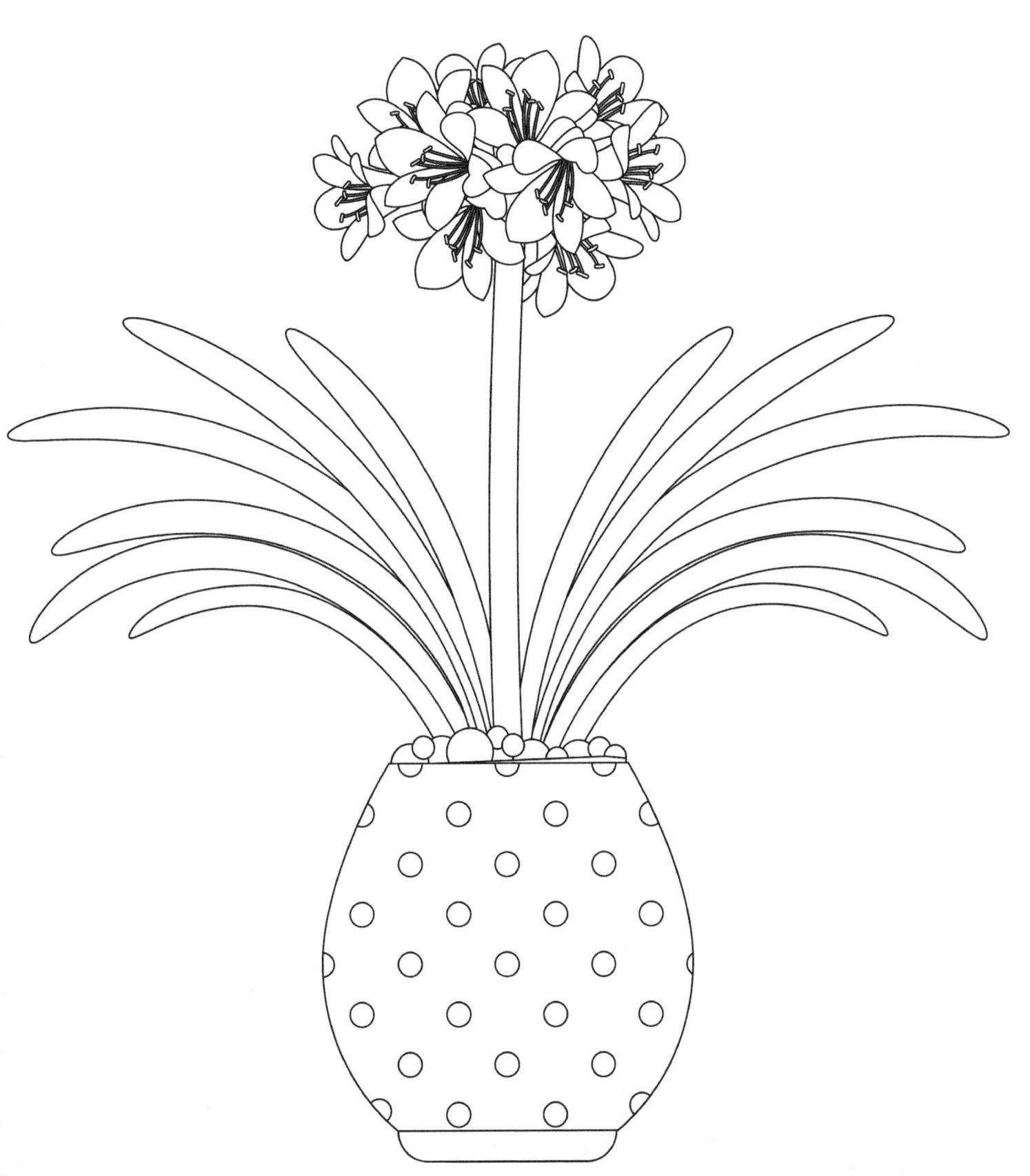

Peanut Cactus

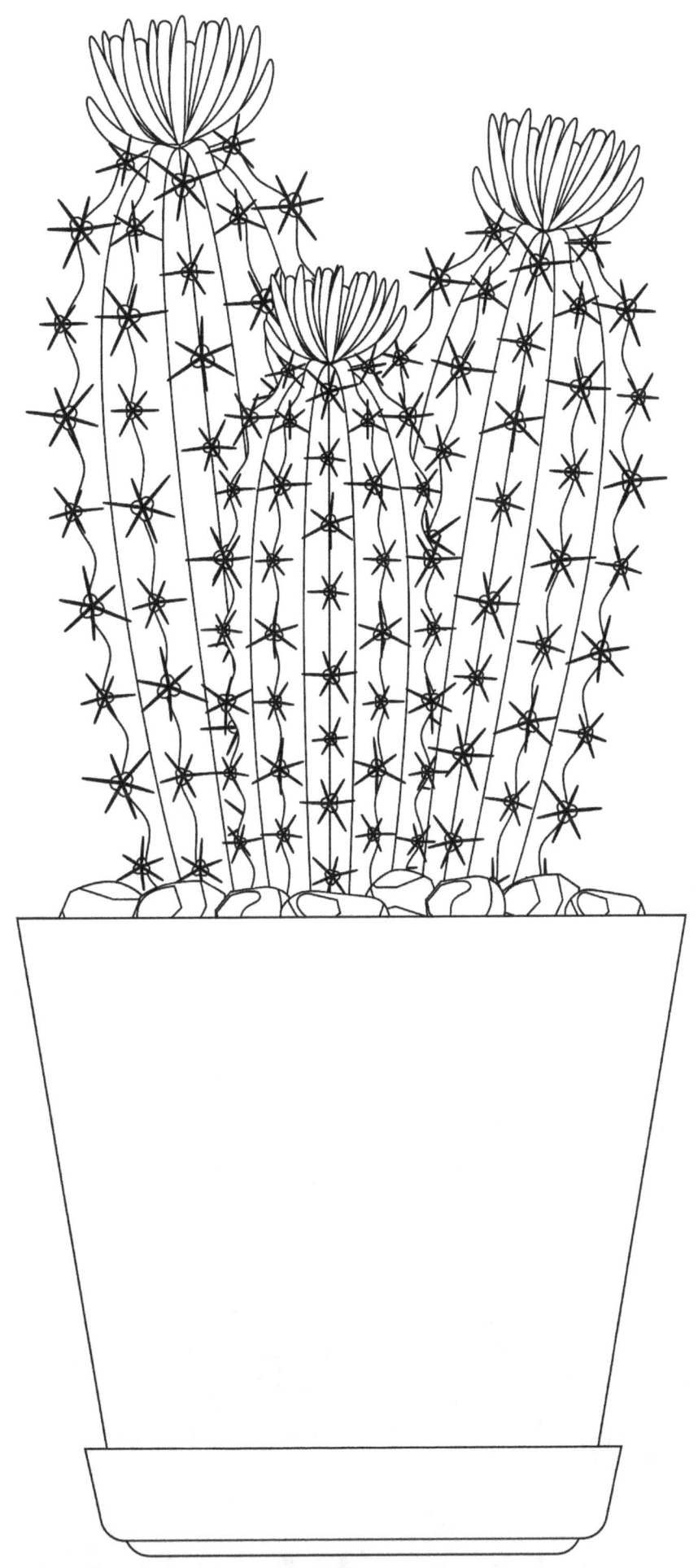

Coleus

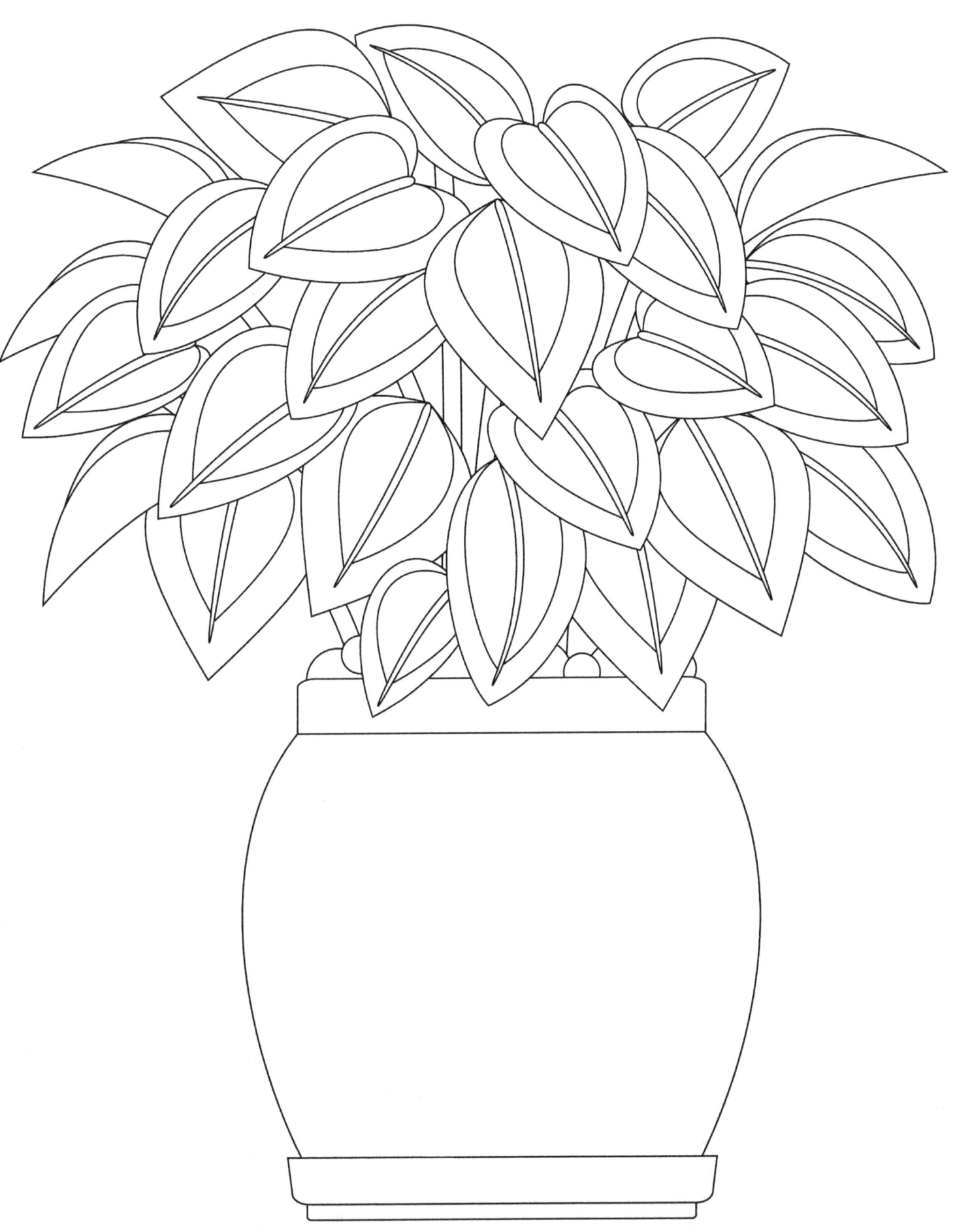

Guzmania

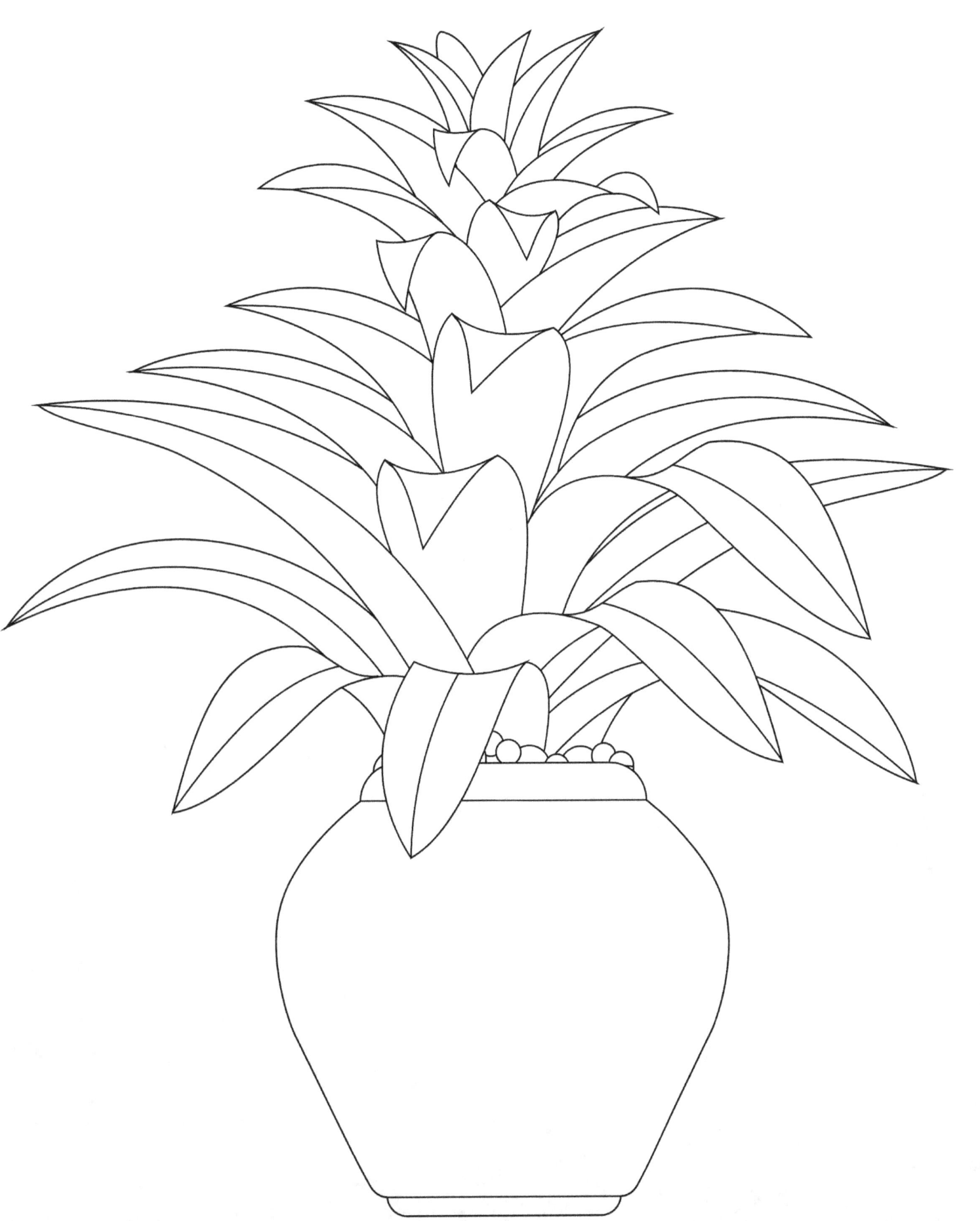

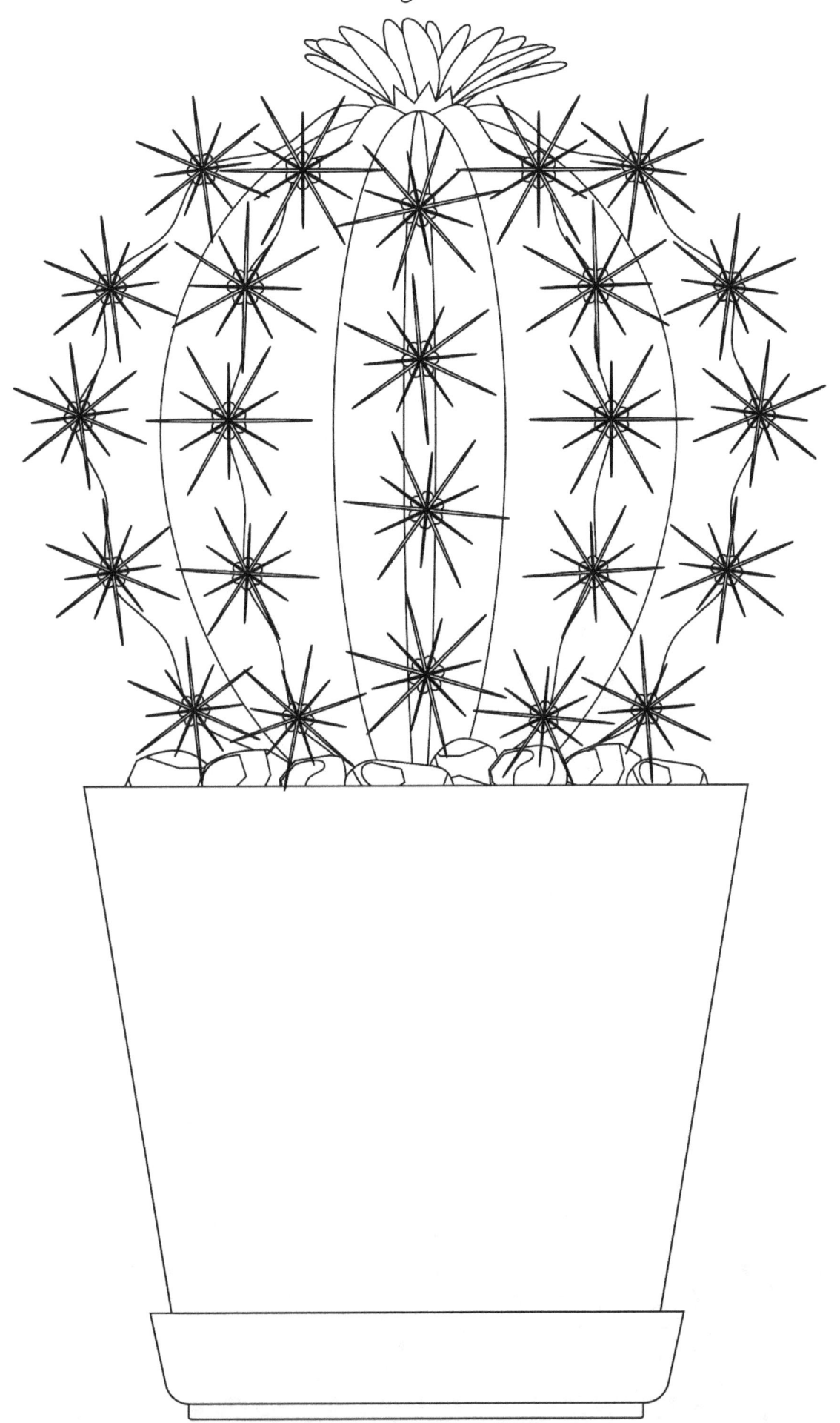

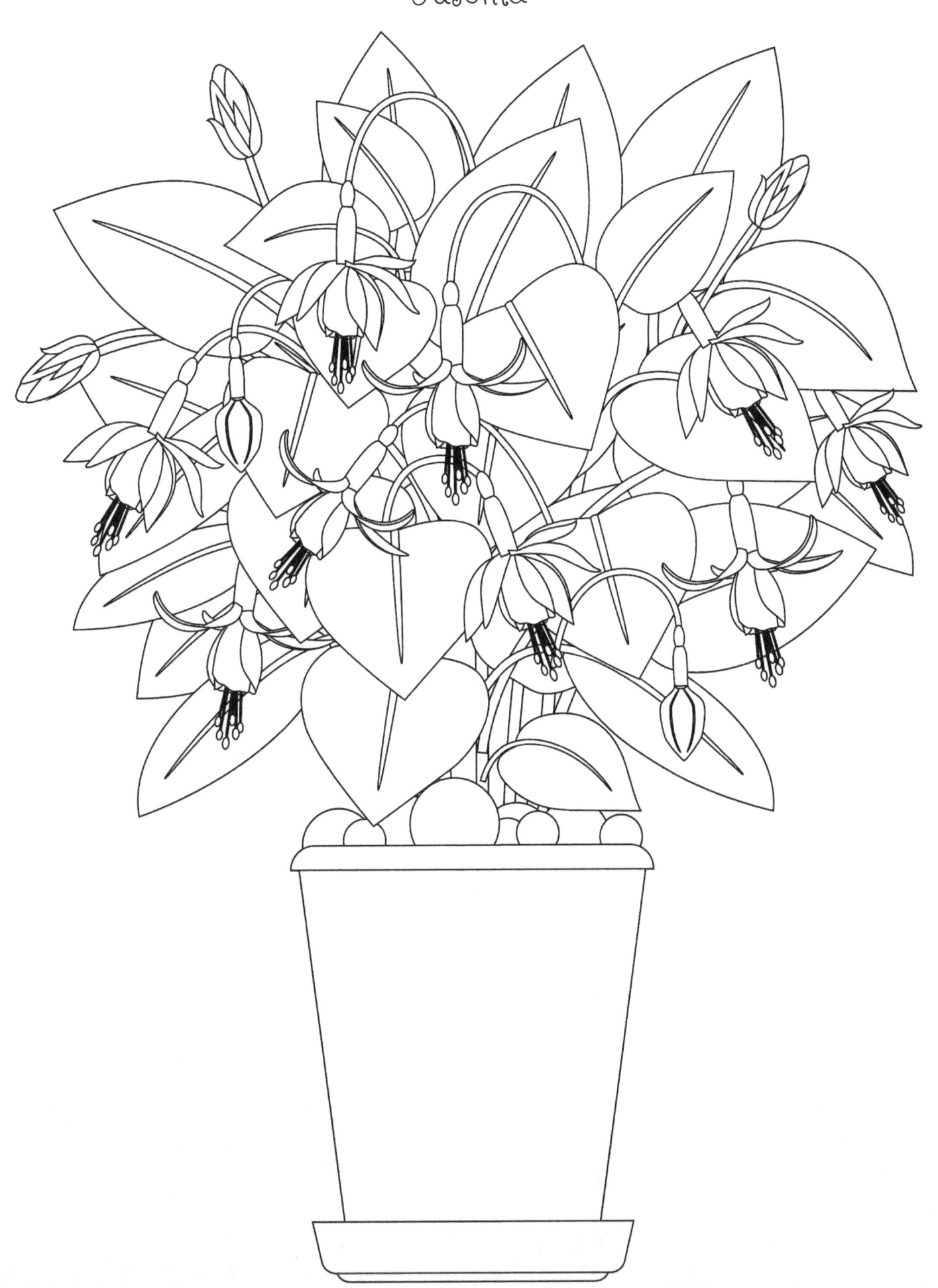

Spiderwort

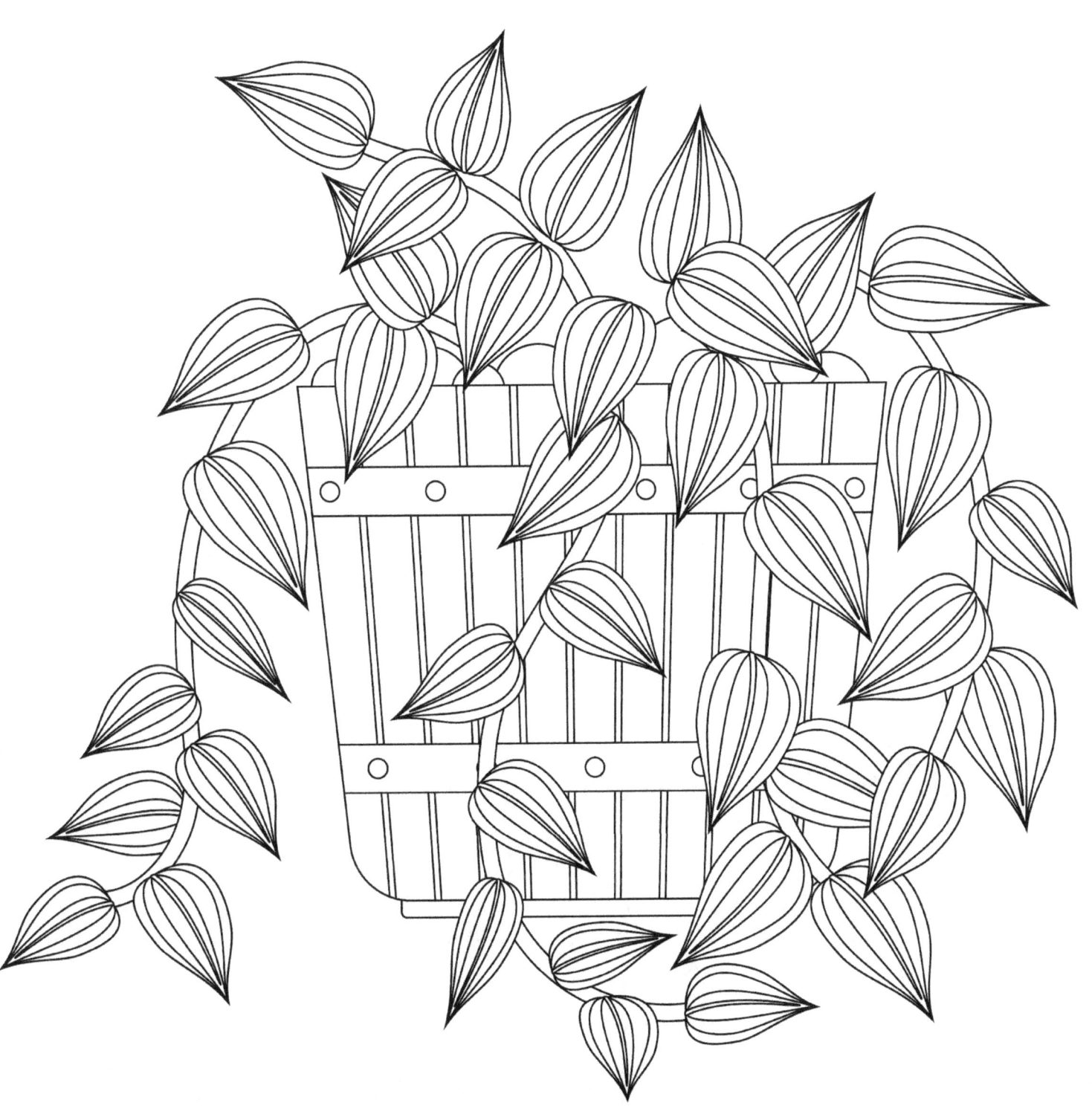

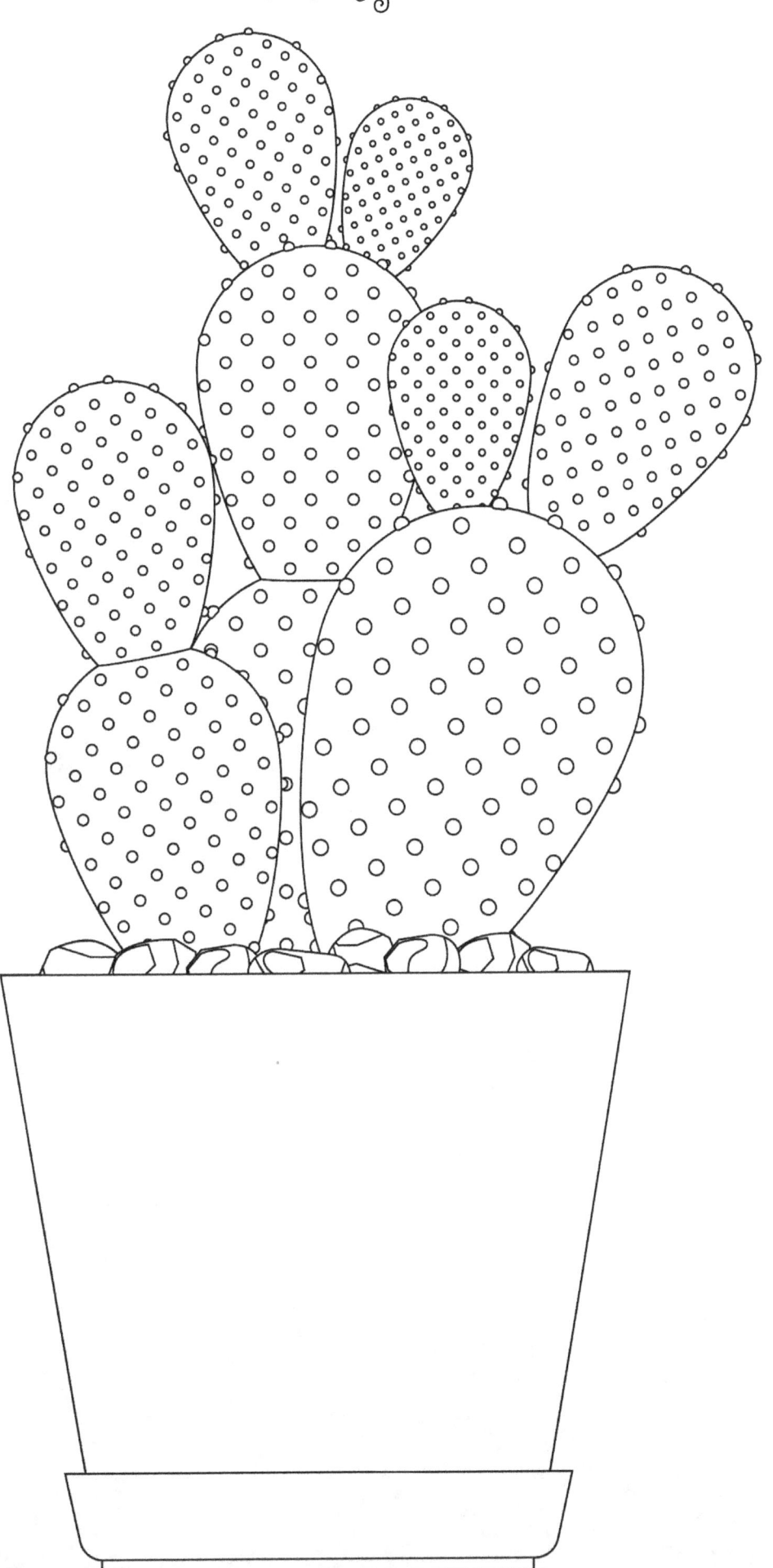

Violet

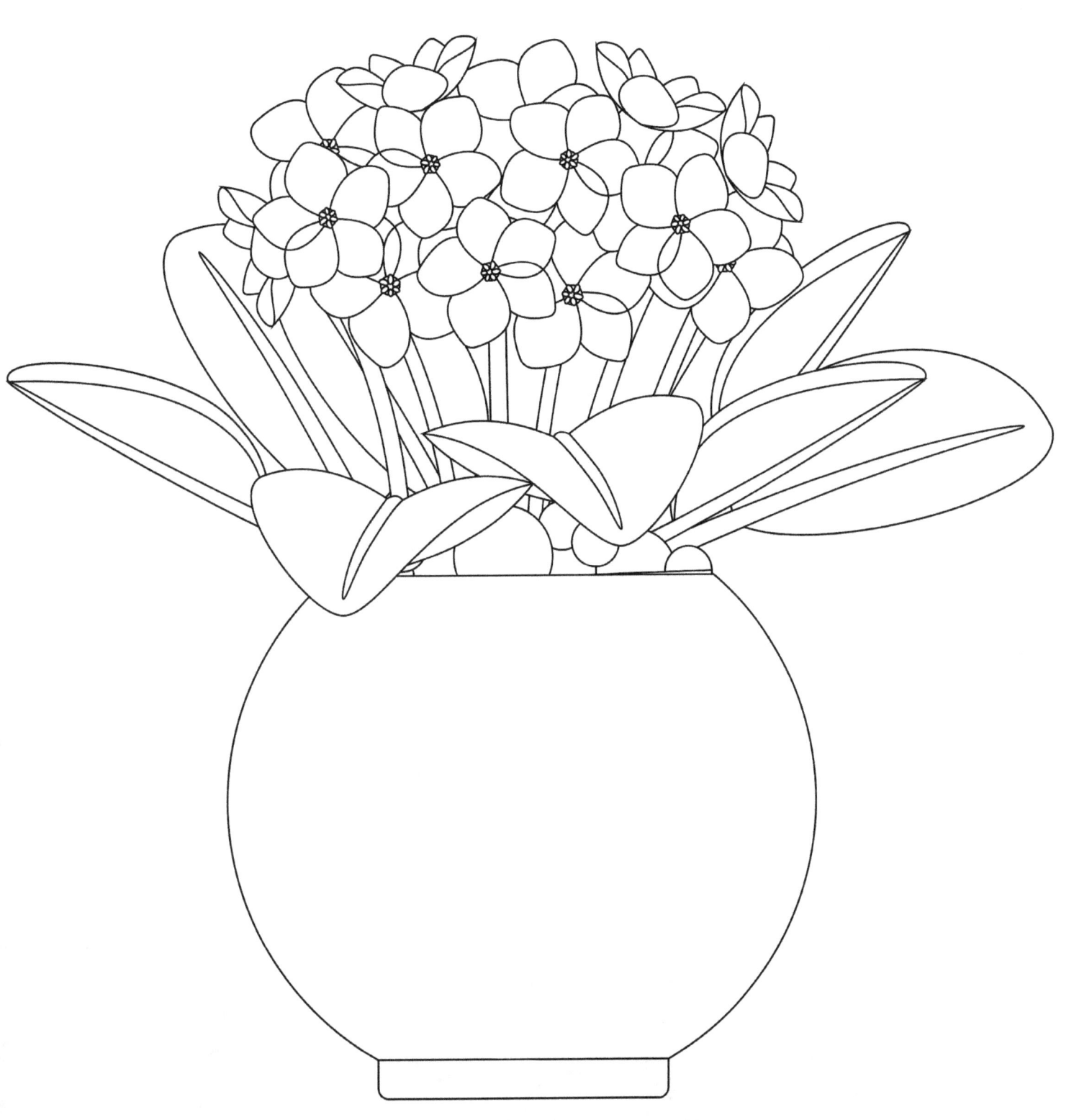

Begonia

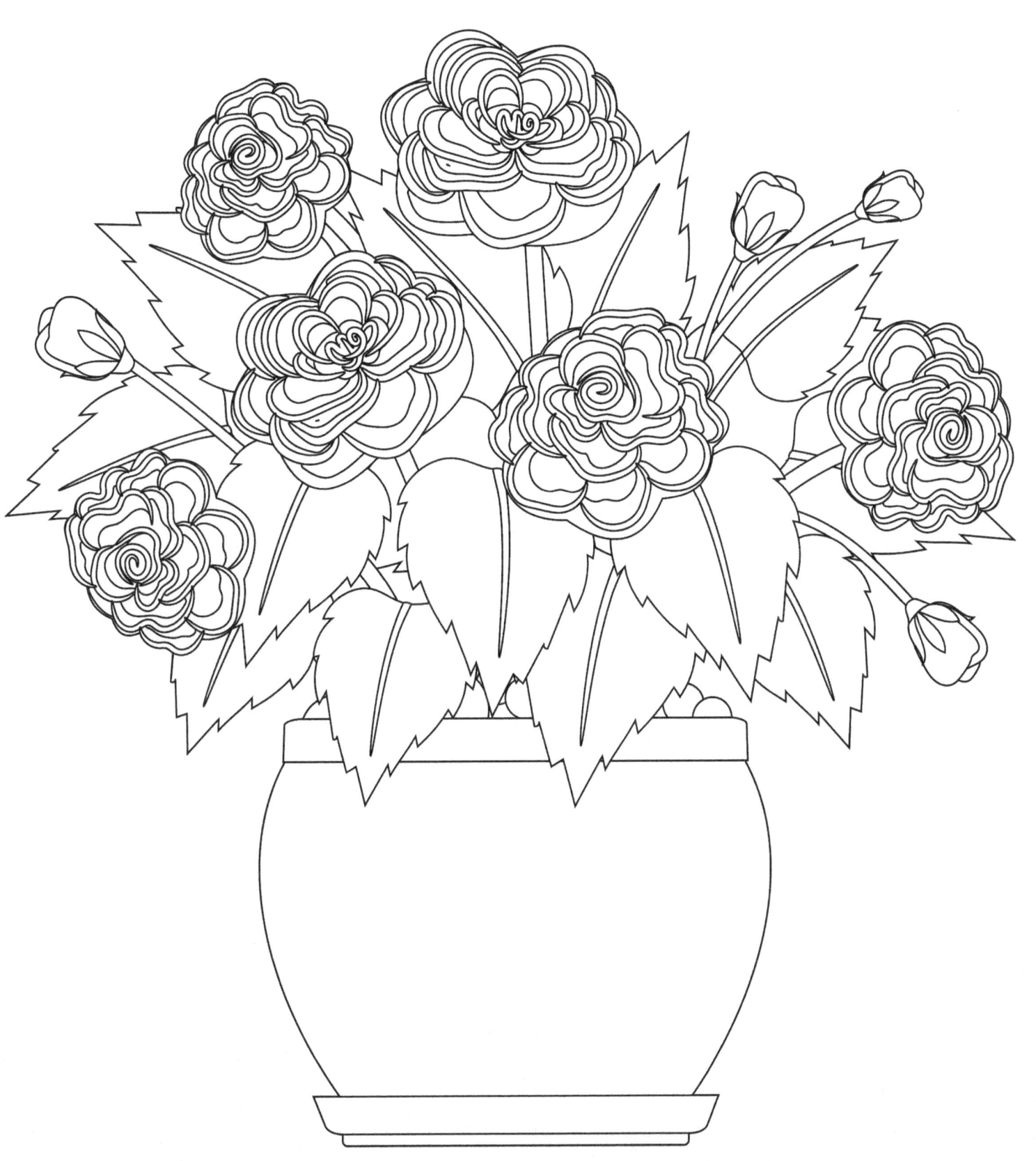

Touch-me-not

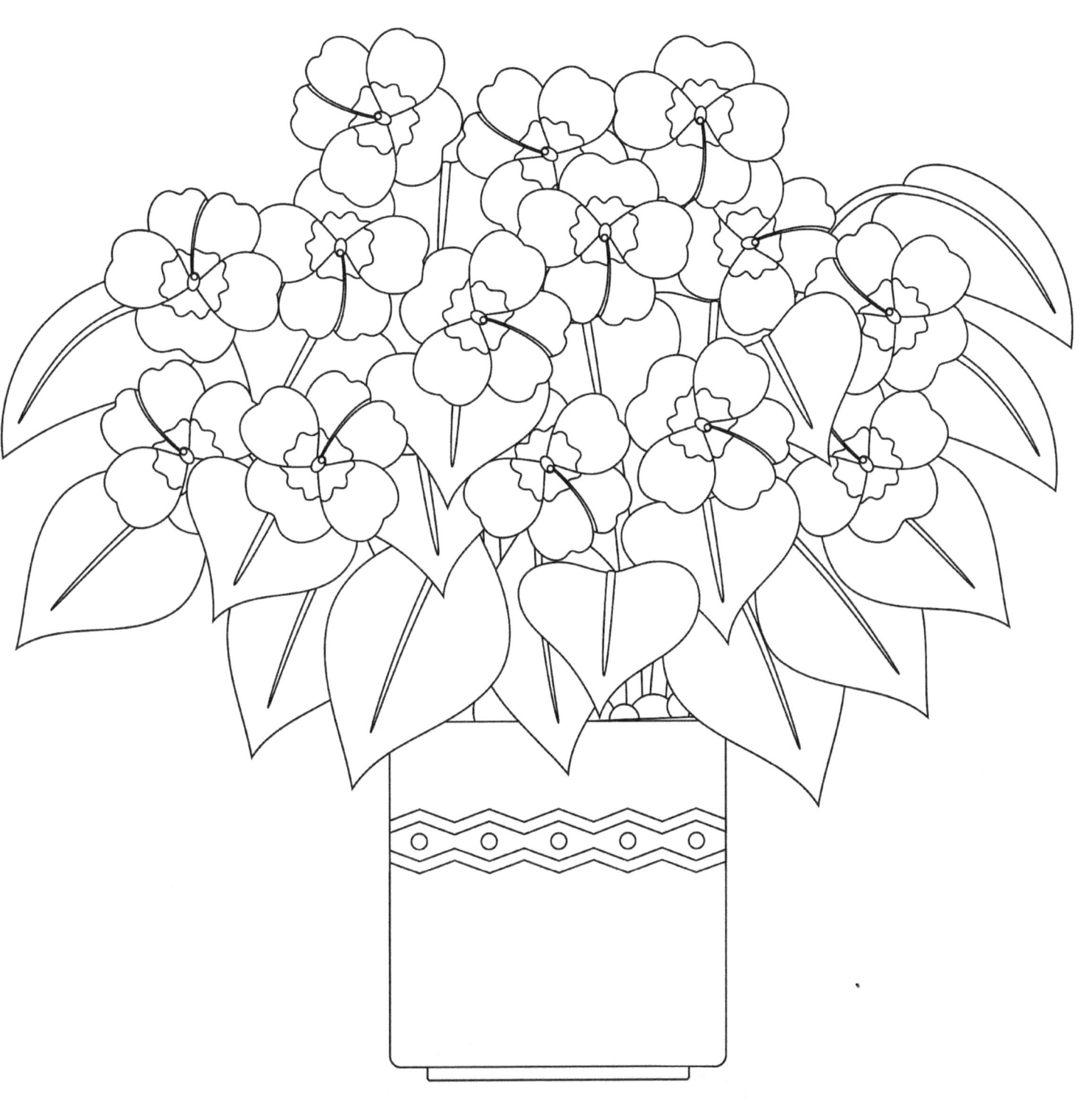

Chin Cactus

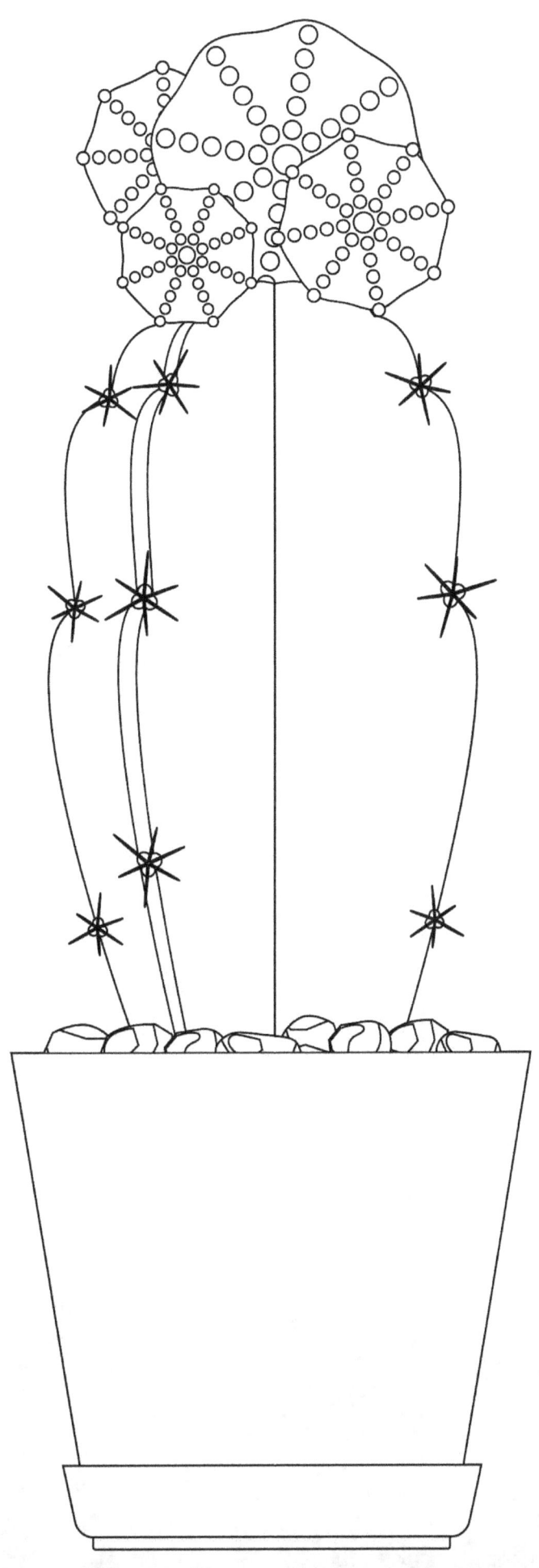

Chinese Evergreens

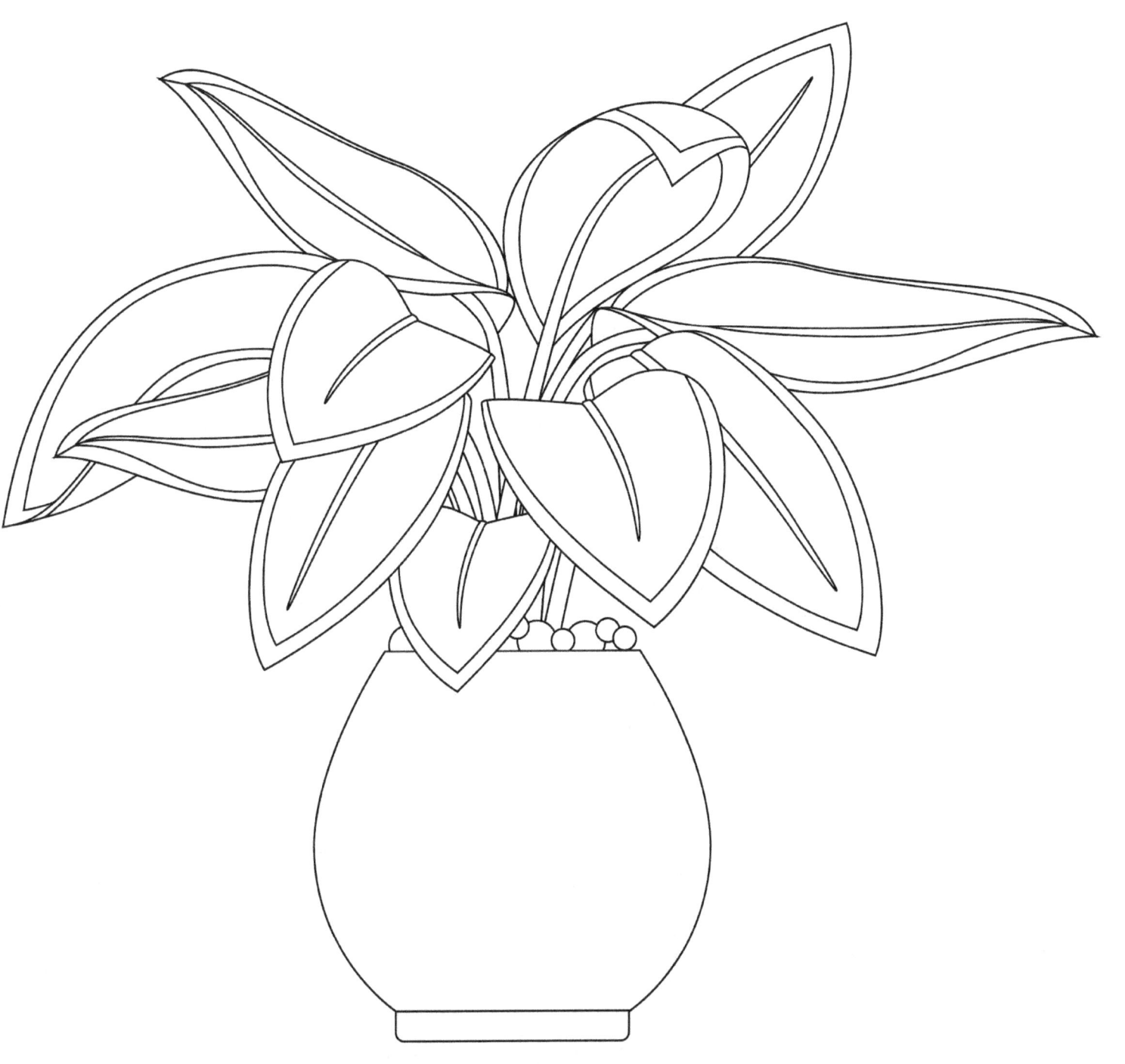

Painter's-palette

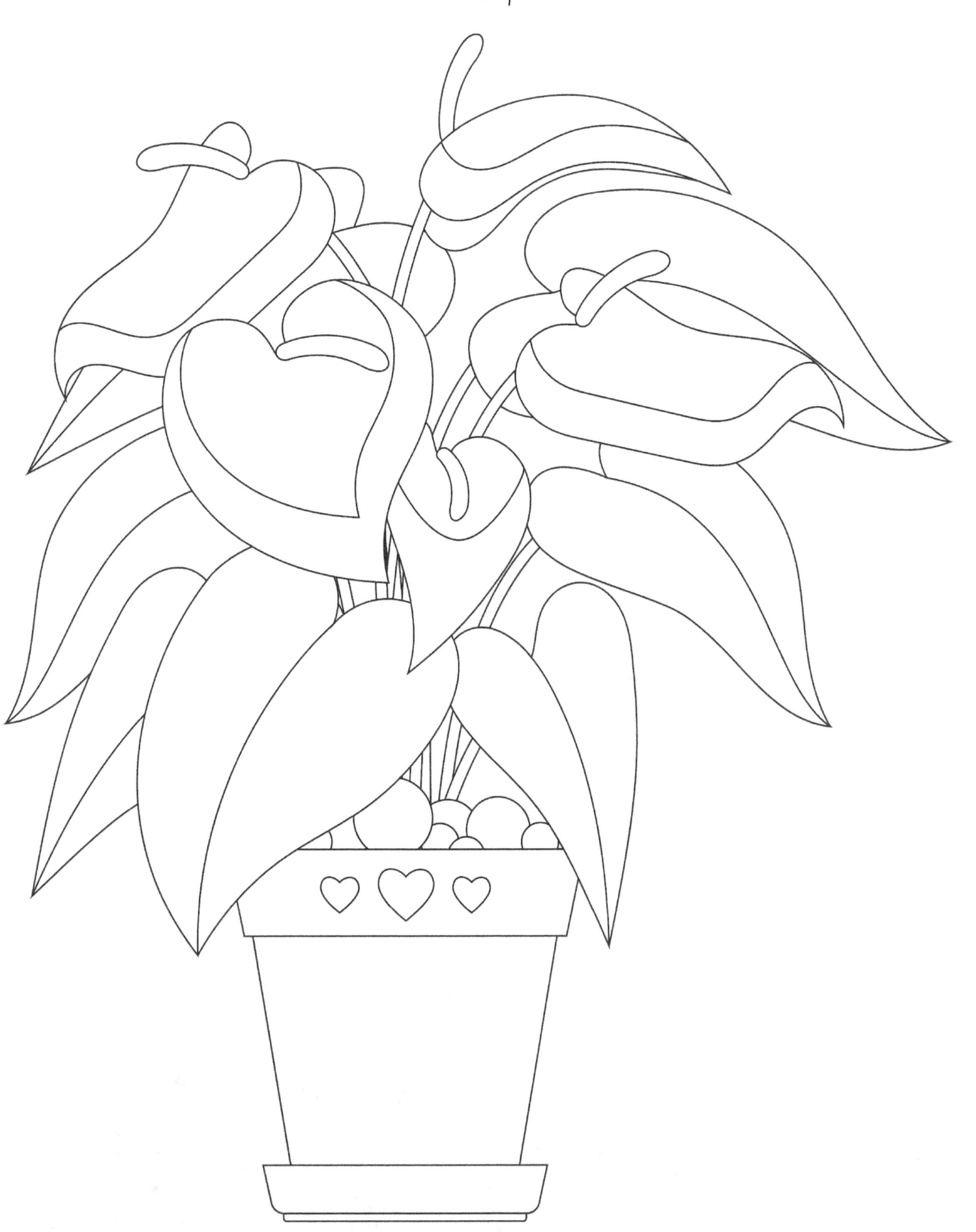

Maidenhair Fern

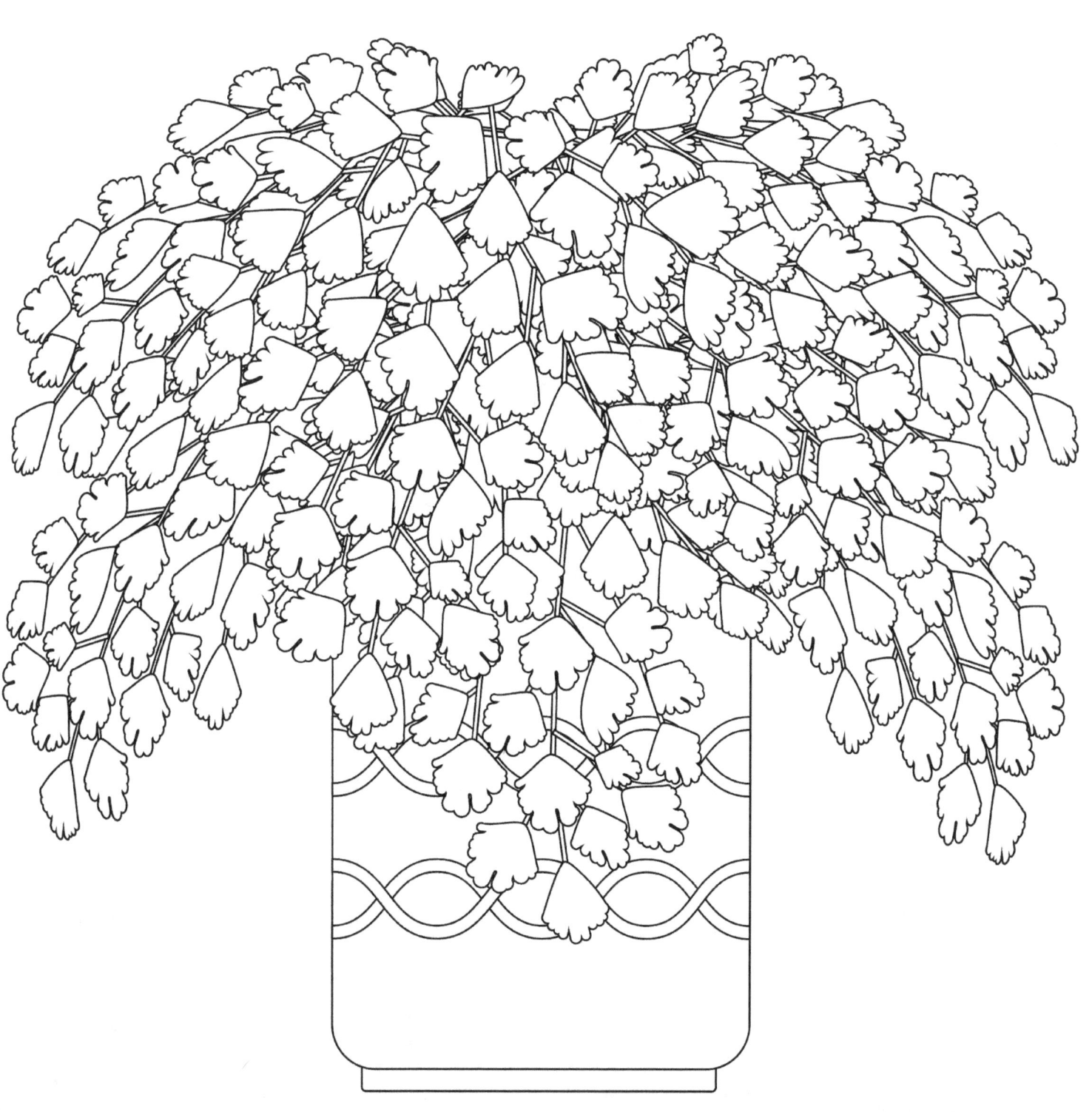

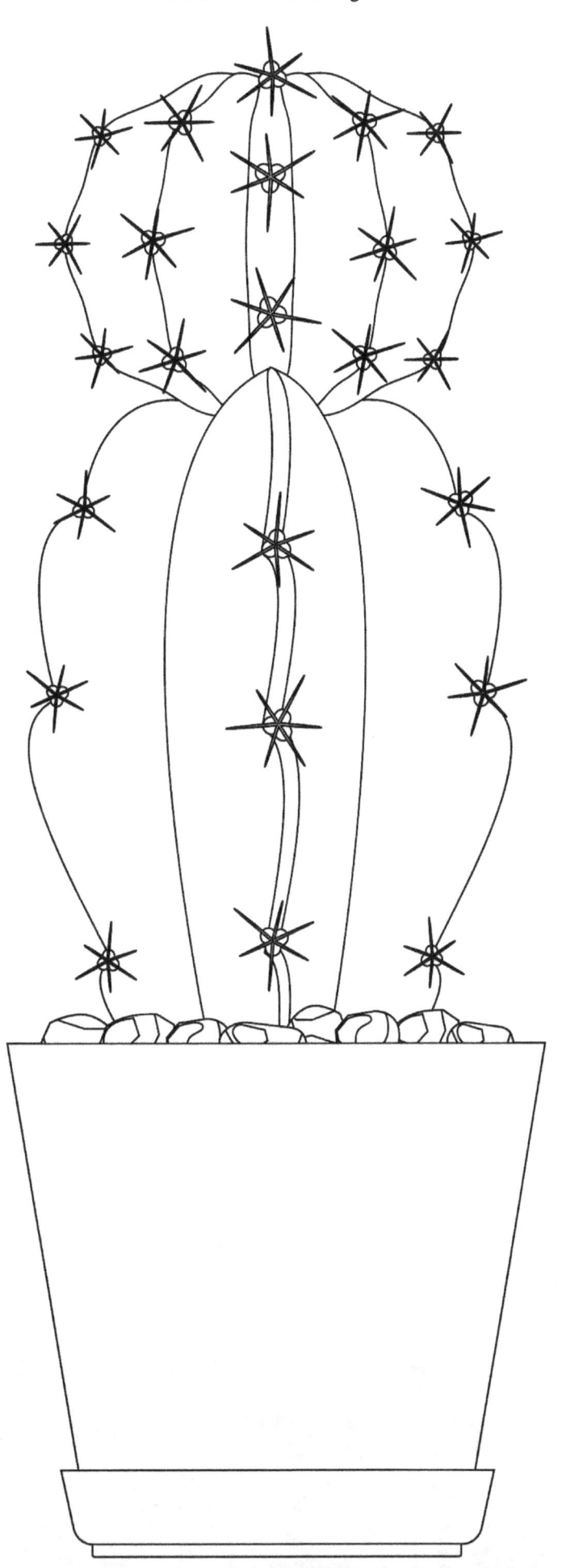
Lizard Skin

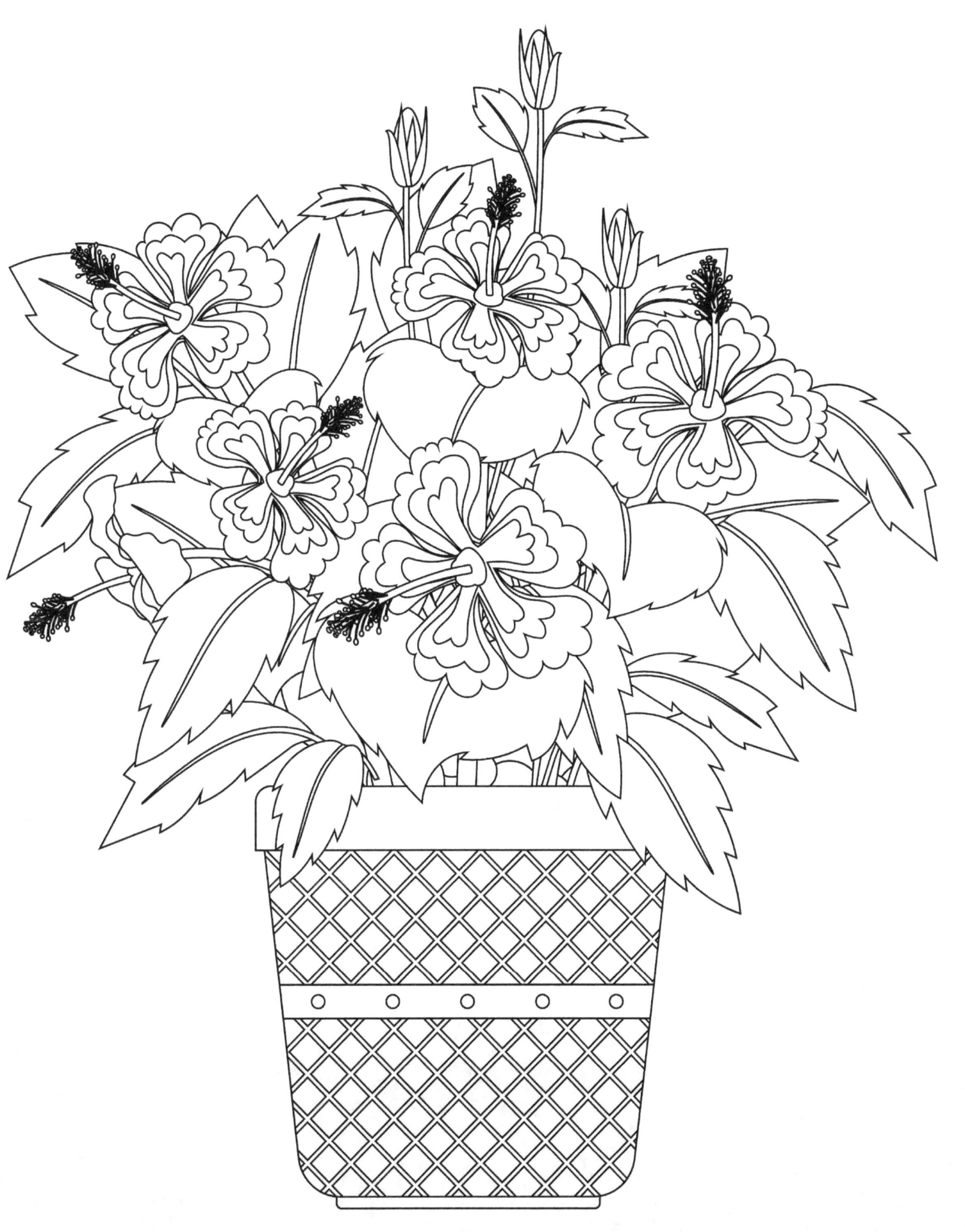

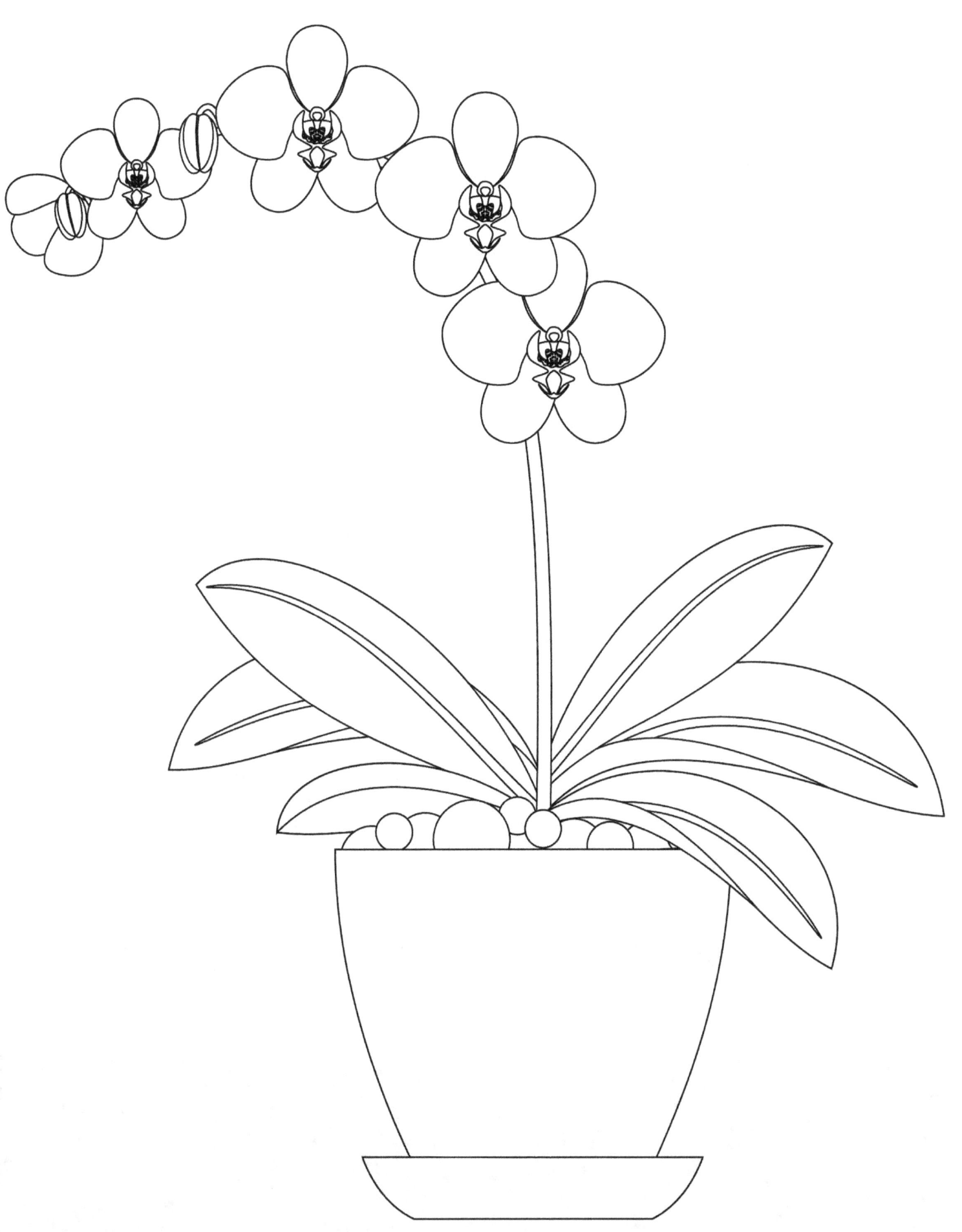

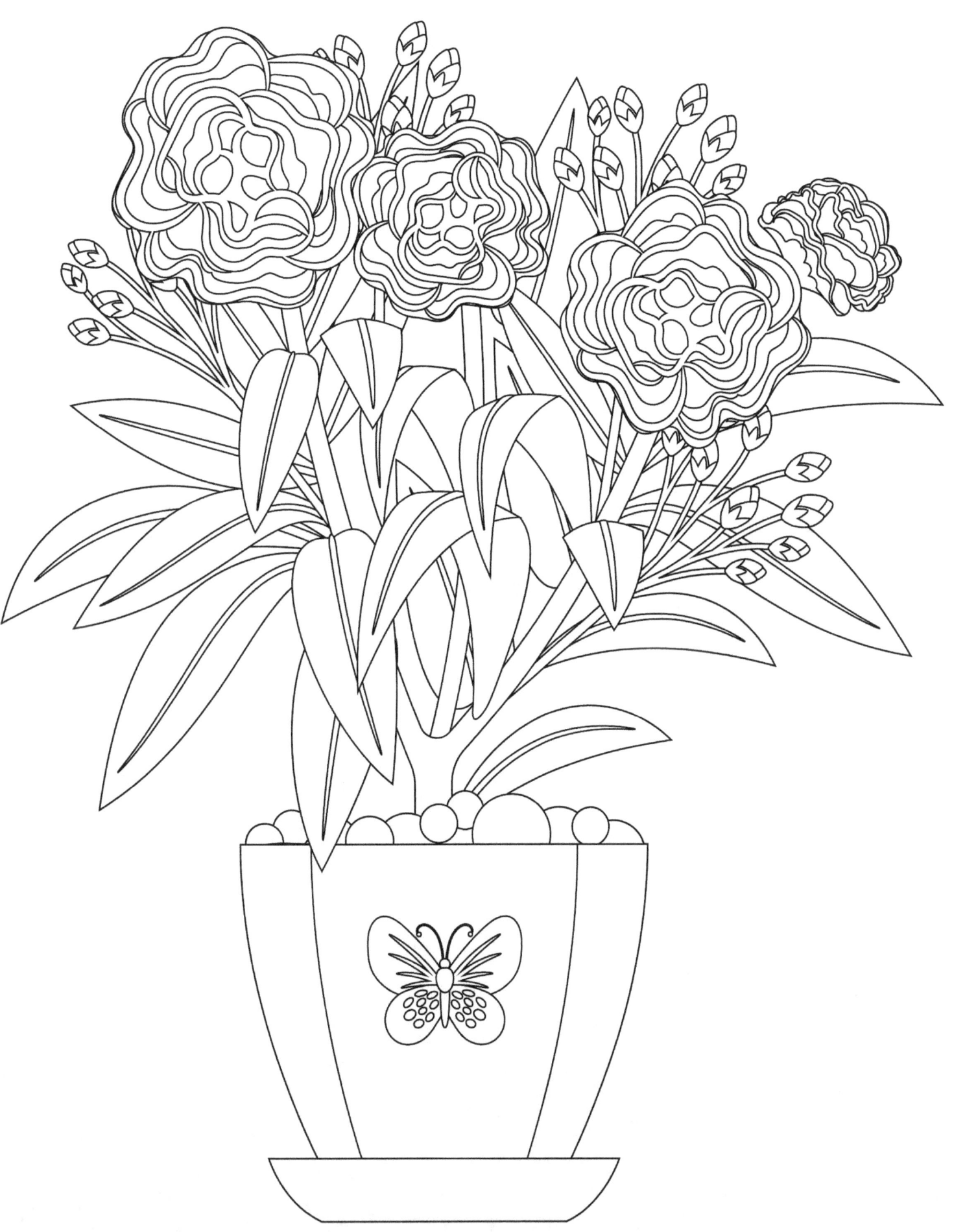

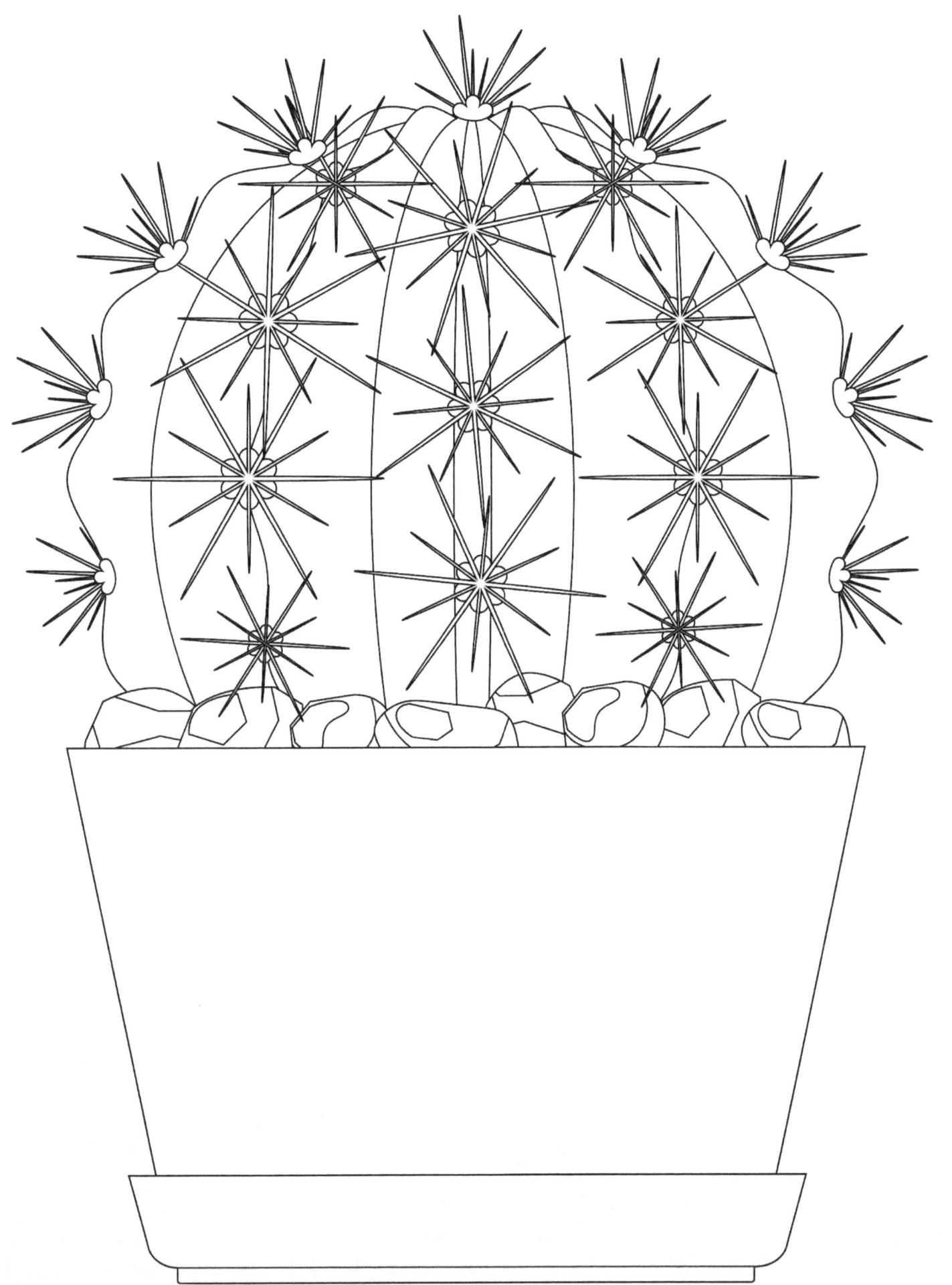

Widow's-thrill

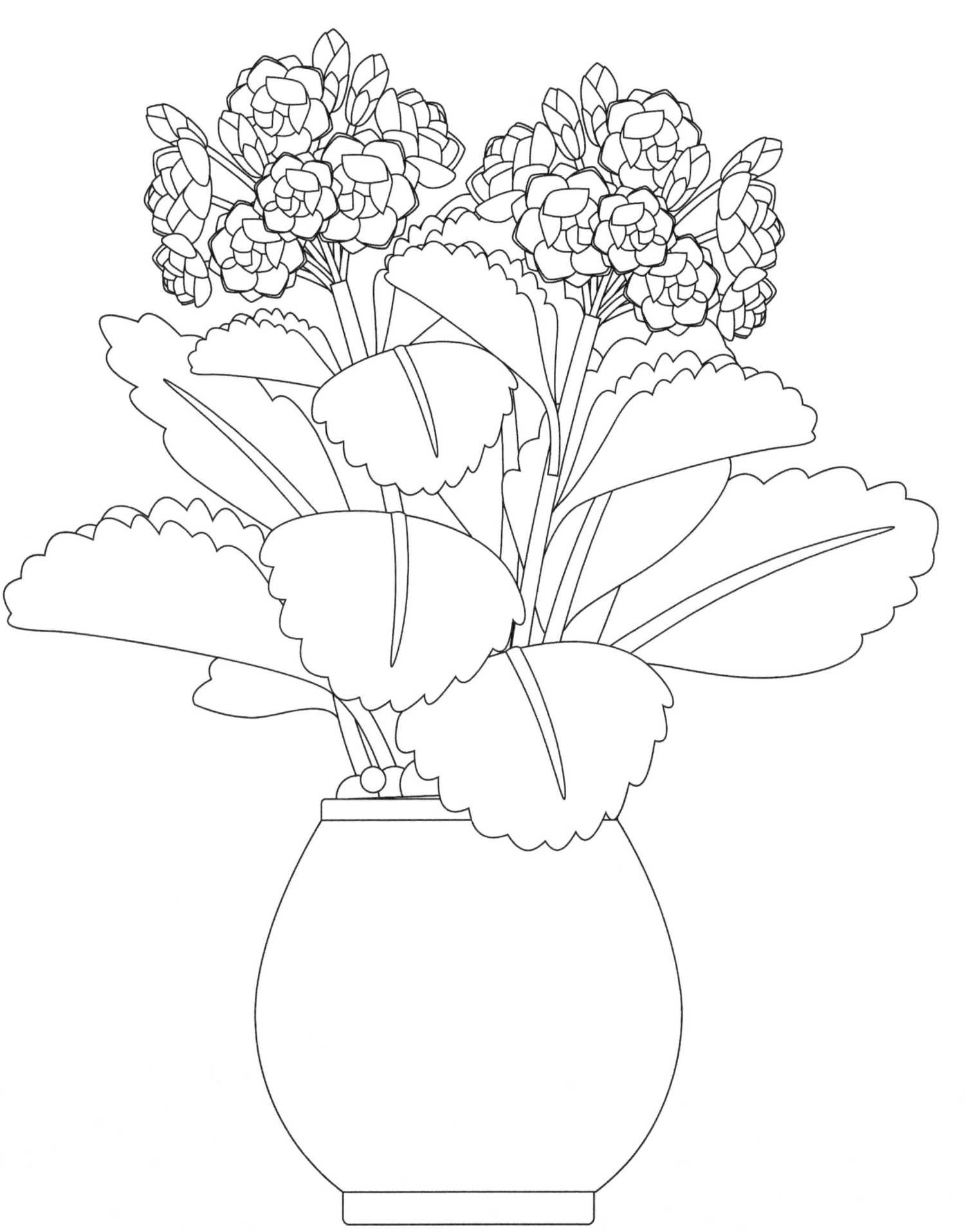

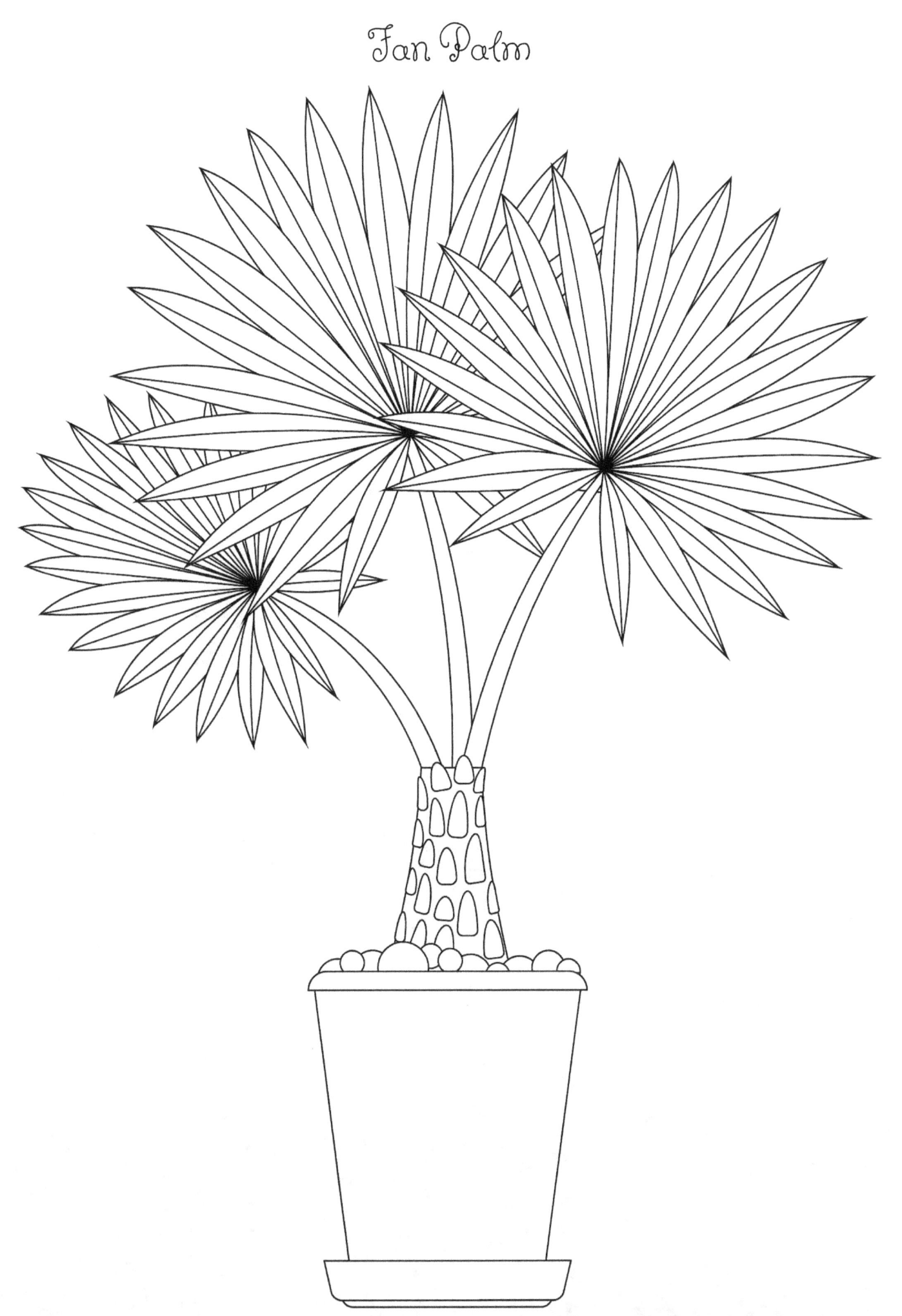

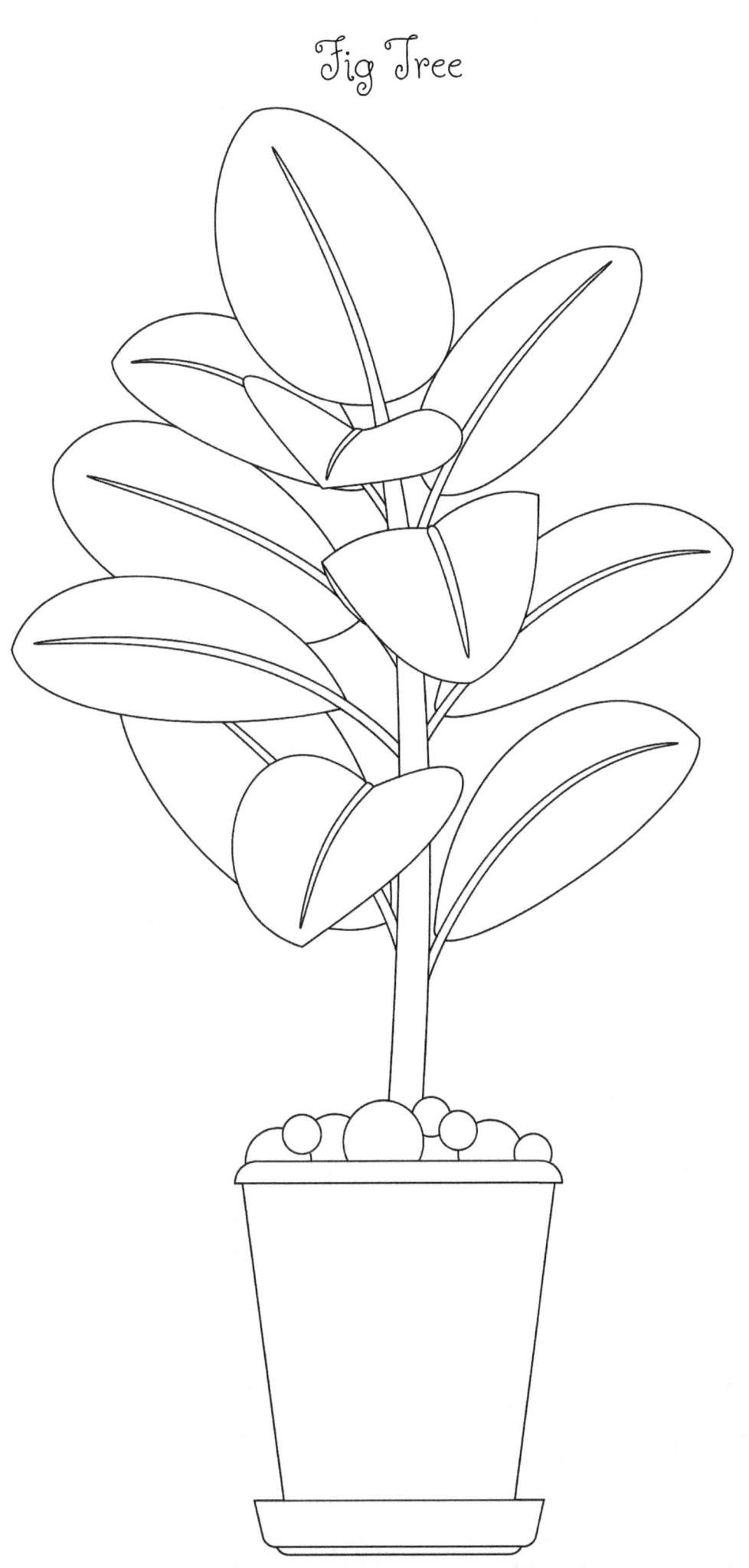

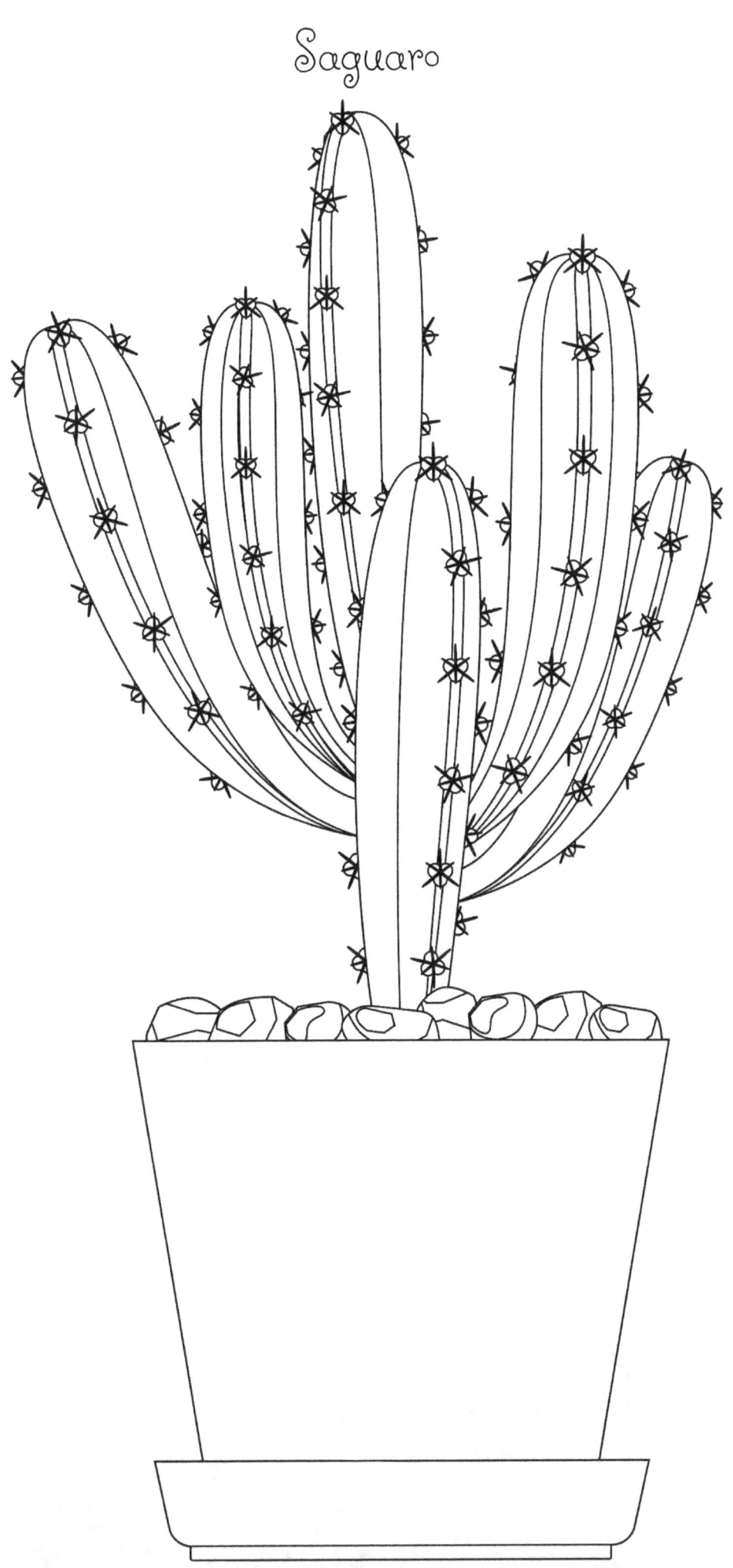

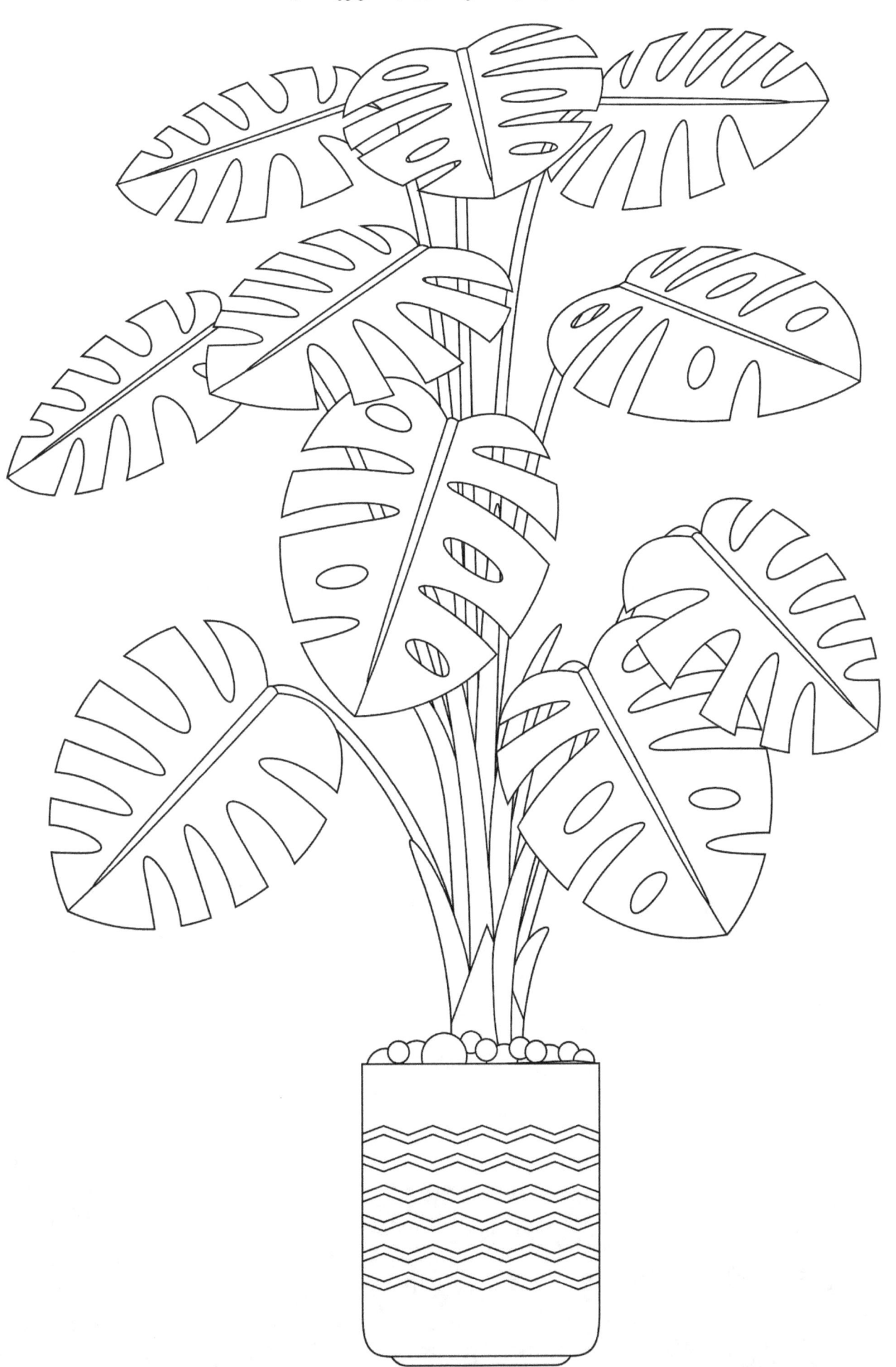

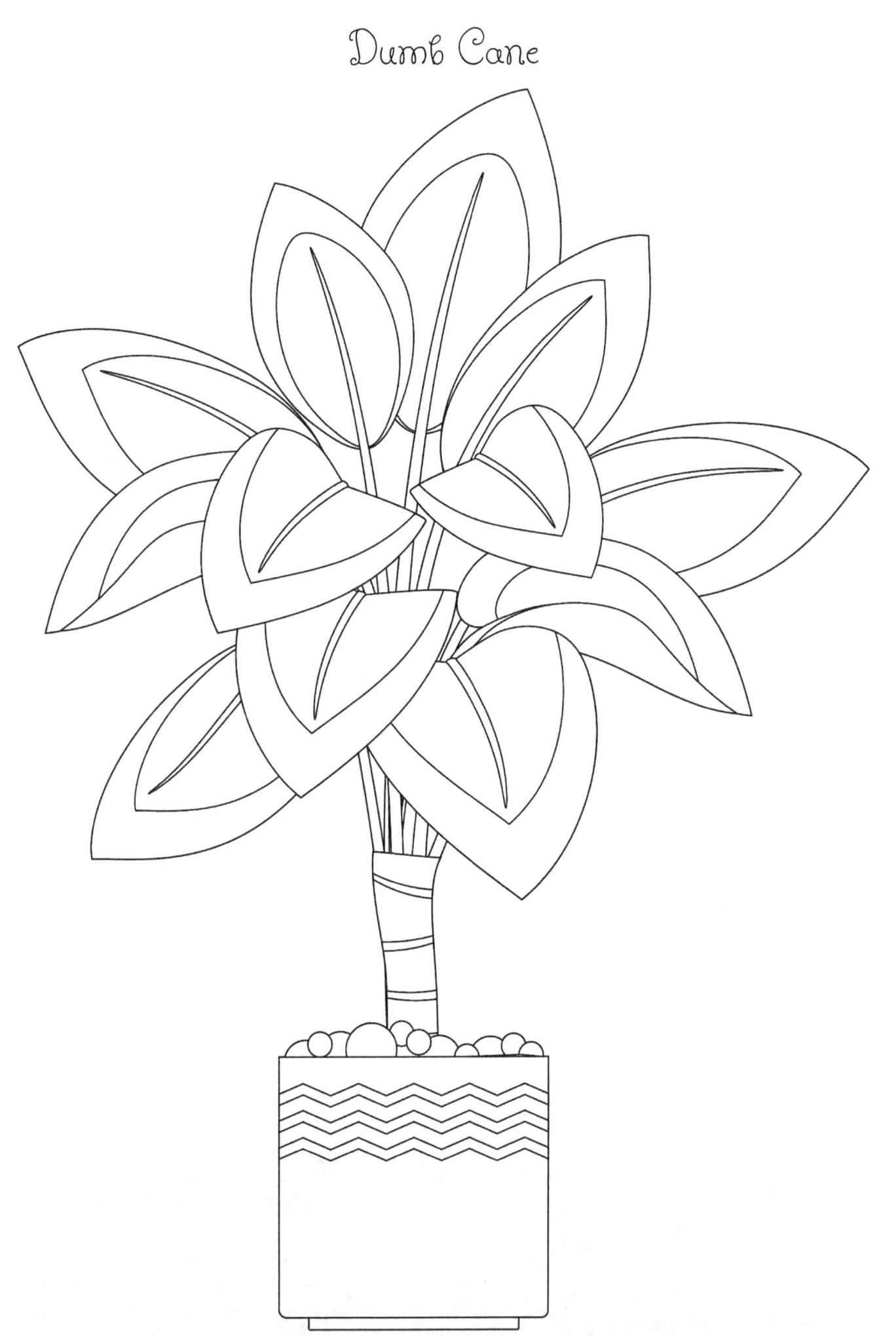

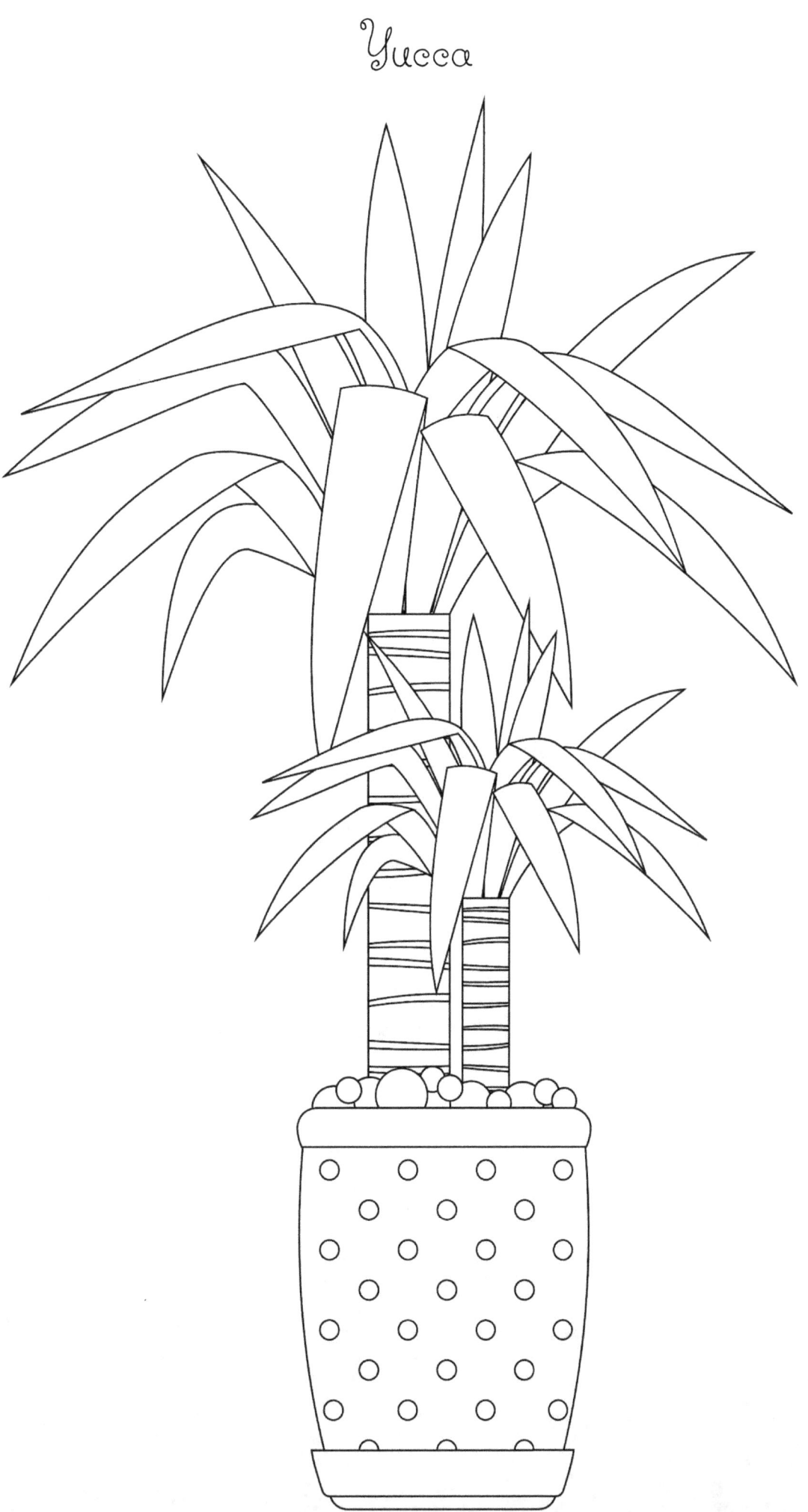

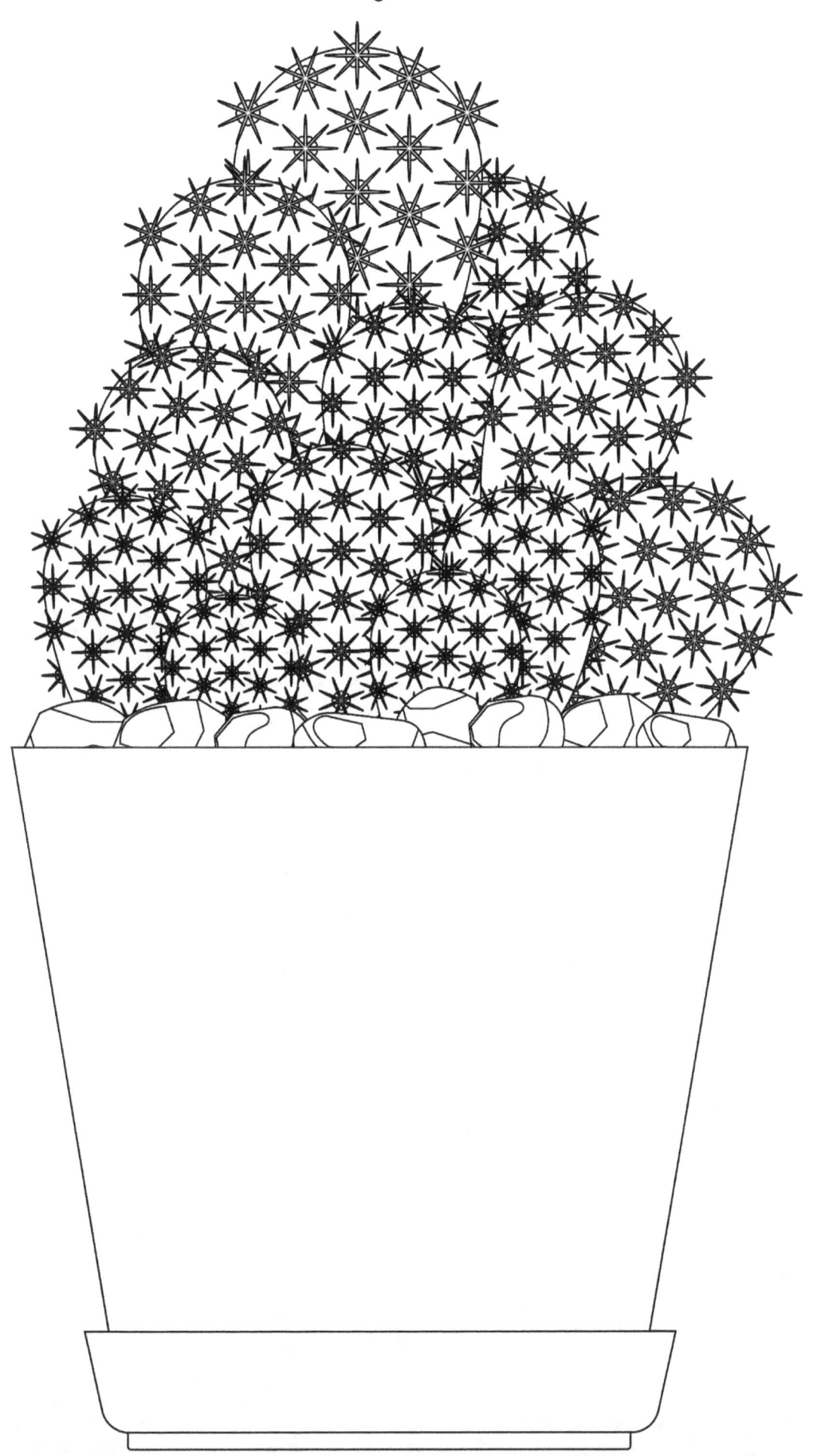

Dracaena

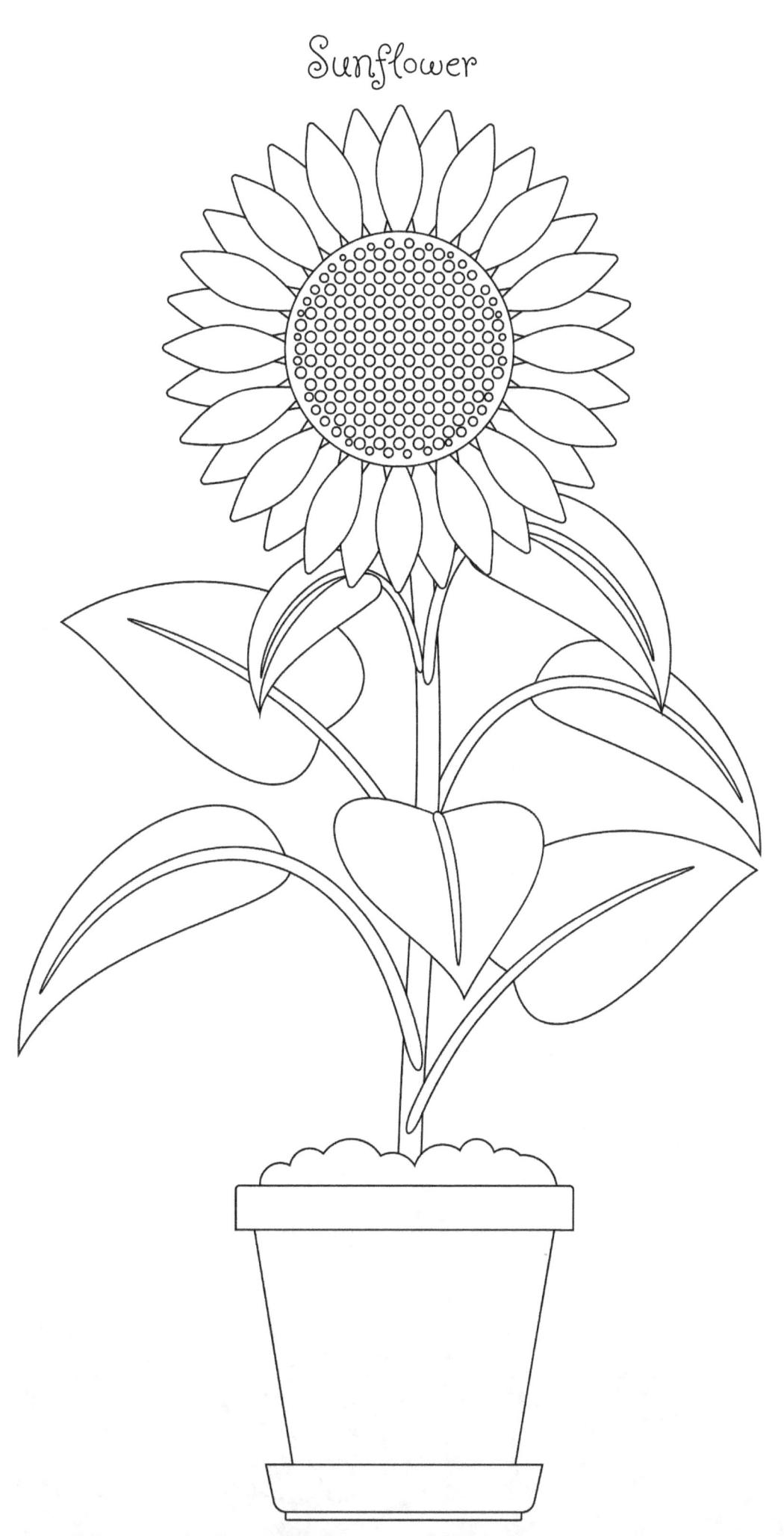

Creme Brulee Agave

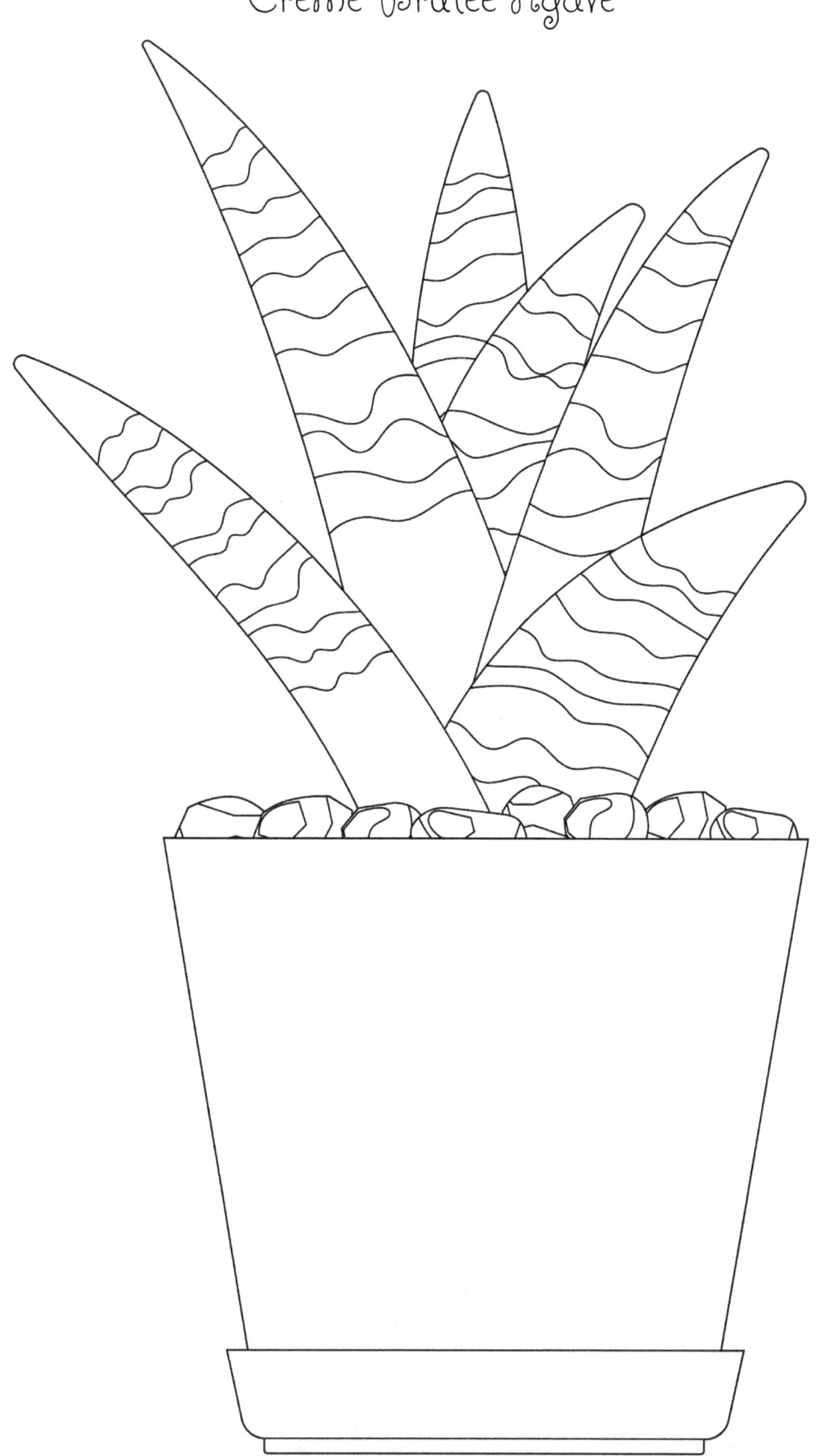

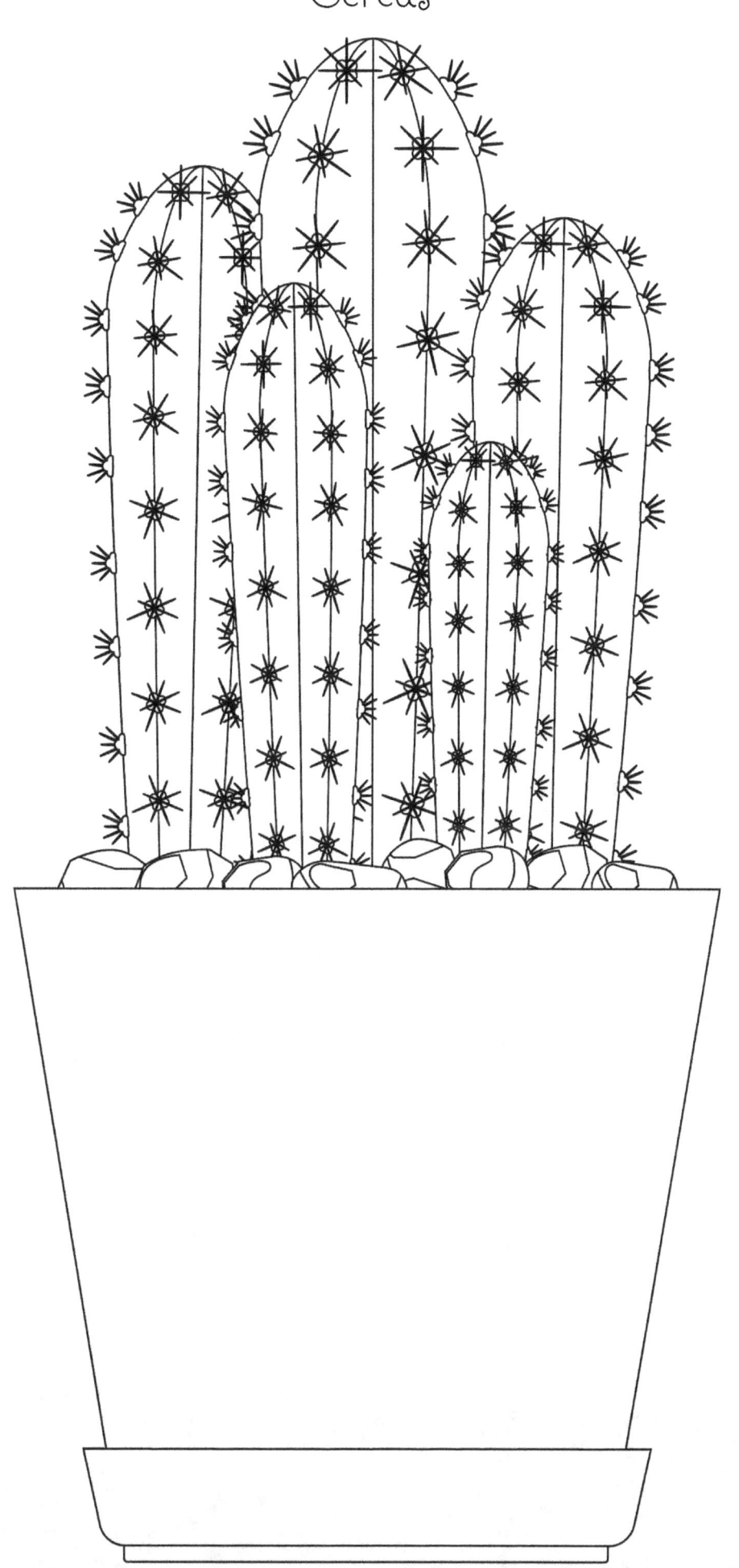

Burro's Tail

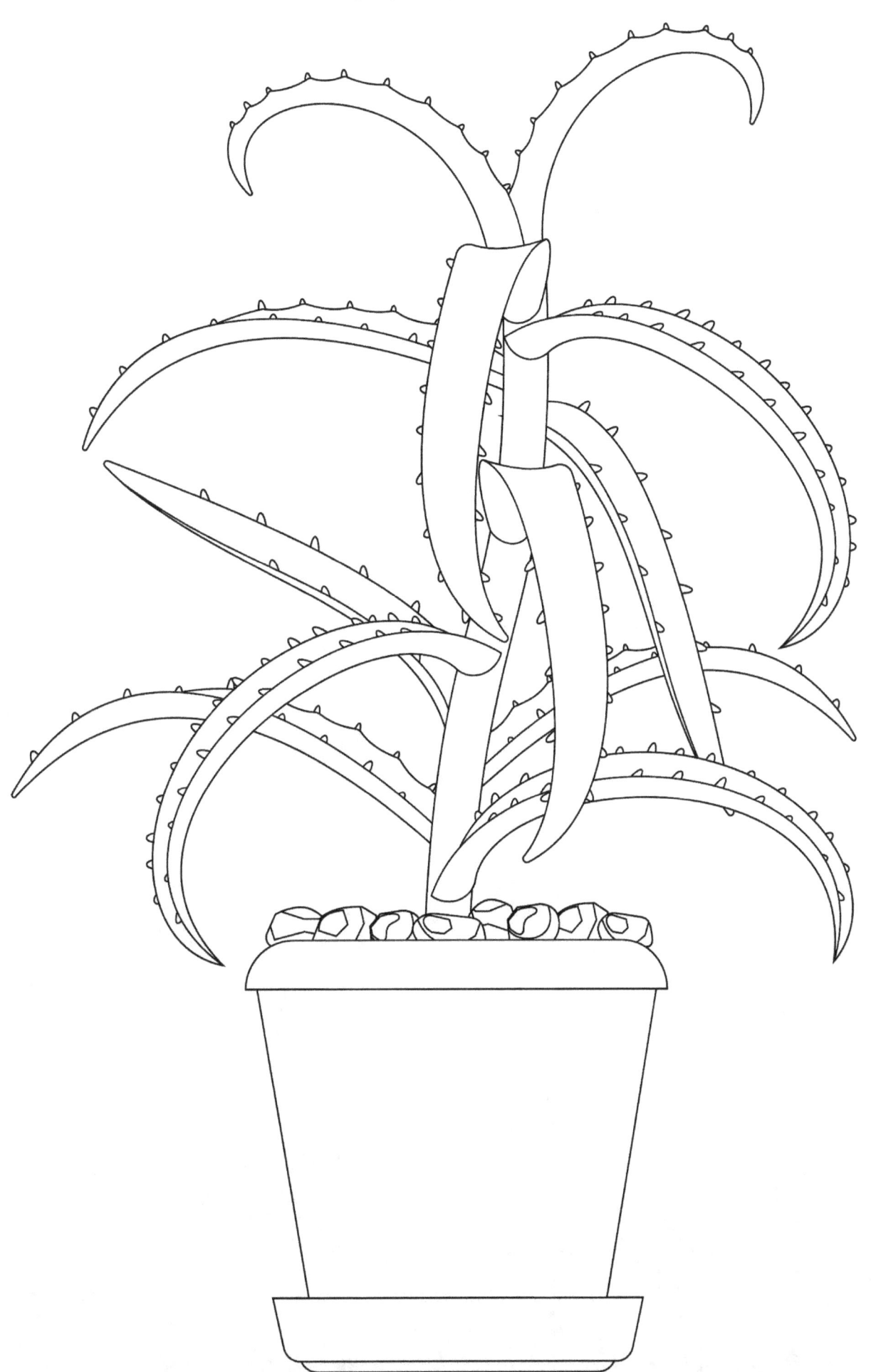

Camellia

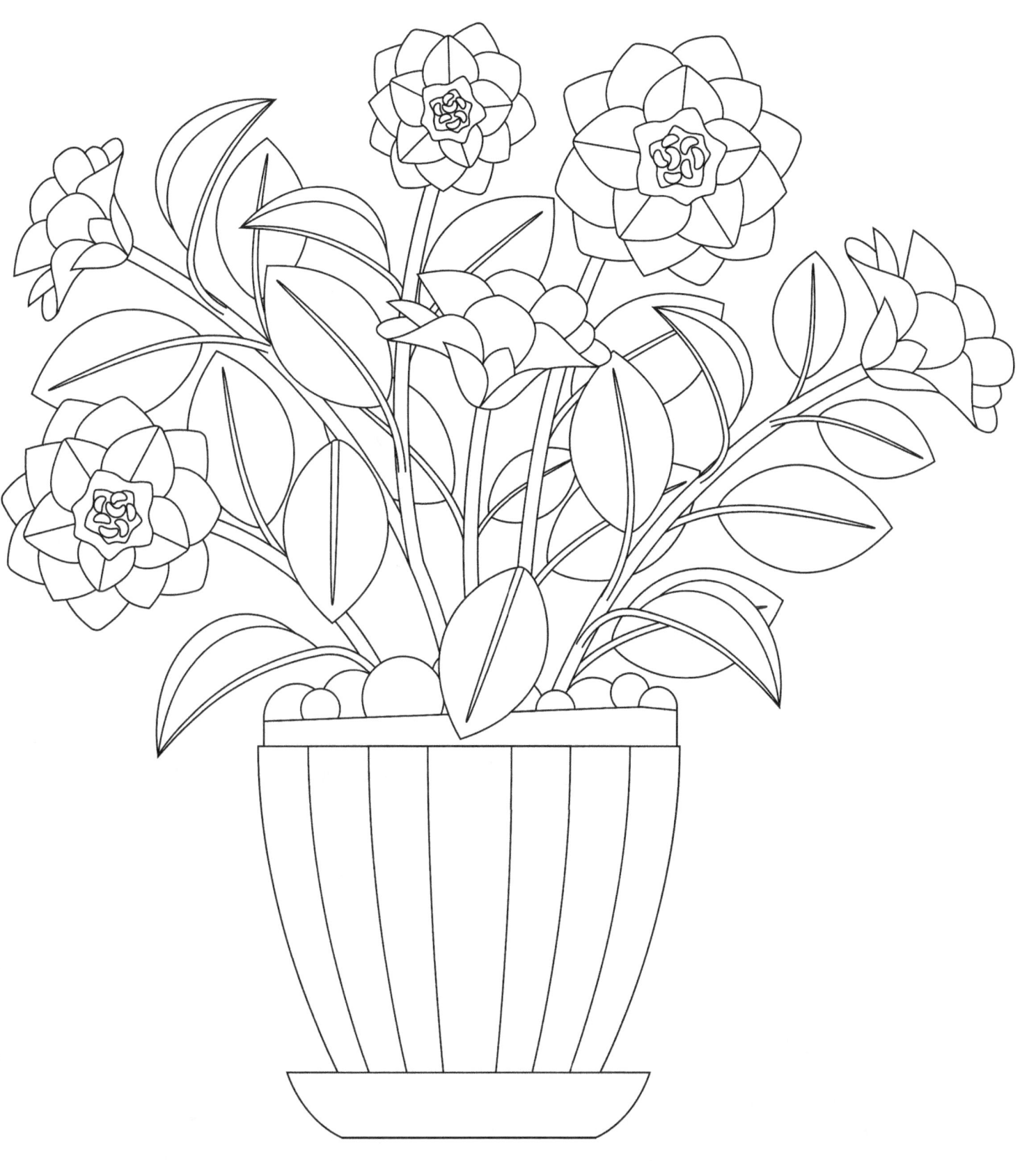

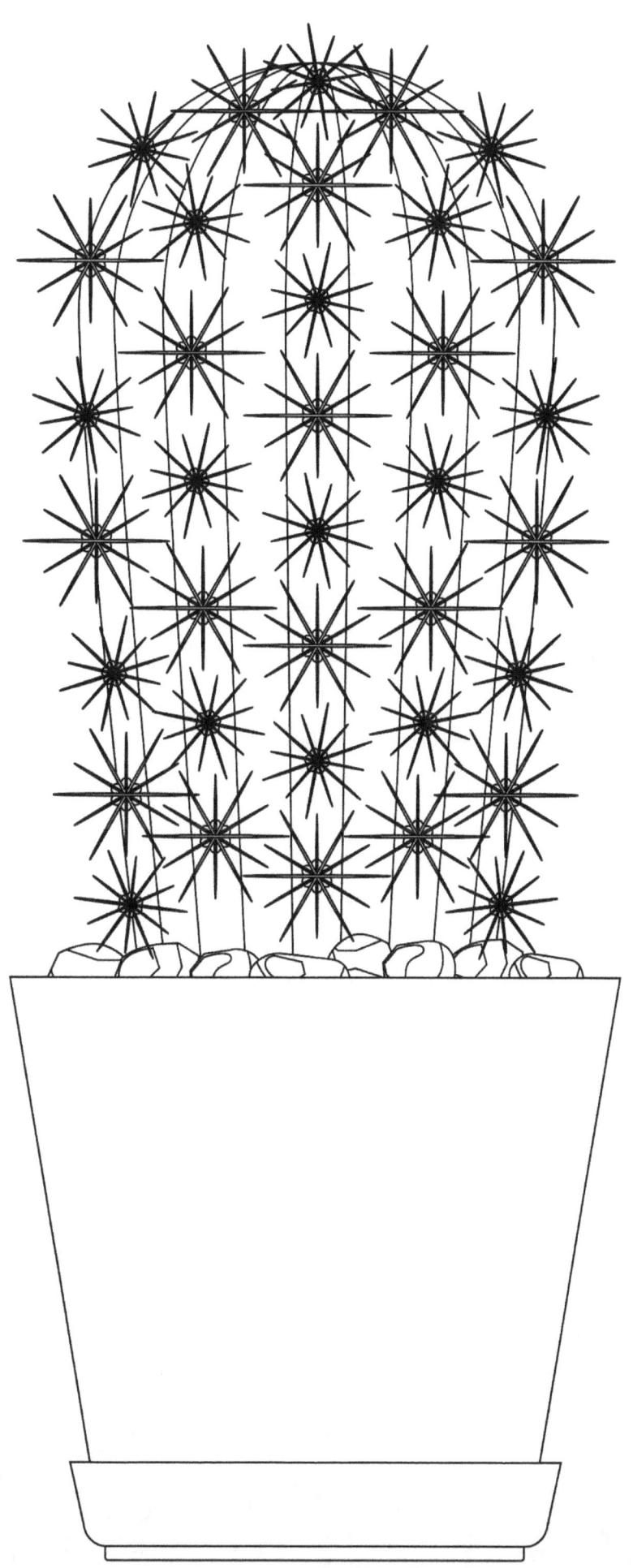

Jade Plant

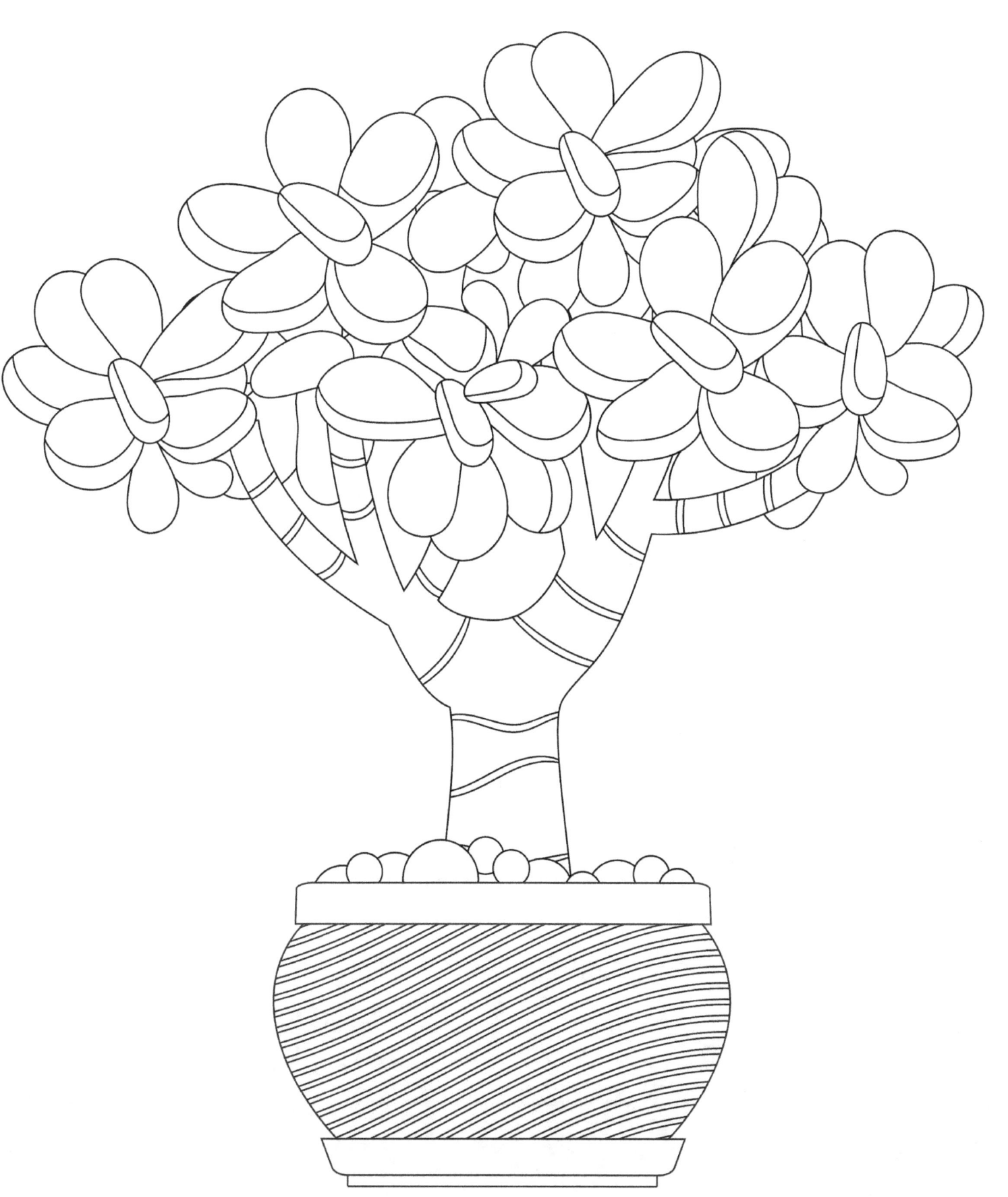